THE
MEDIEVAL
CHURCH

D1569367

ROLAND H. BAINTON †

Professor Emeritus of Ecclesiastical History
Yale University

THE ANVIL SERIES

under the general editorship of

LOUIS L. SNYDER

ROBERT E. KRIEGER PUBLISHING COMPANY
MALABAR, FLORIDA

Original Edition   1962
Reprint Edition   1979

Printed and Published by
ROBERT E. KRIEGER PUBLISHING COMPANY, INC.
KRIEGER DRIVE
MALABAR, FLORIDA 32950

Copyright © 1962 by
Ronald H. Bainton
Reprinted by Arrangement with
D. VAN NOSTRAND COMPANY, INC.

Printed in the United States of America

Library of Congress Cataloging in Publication Data

Bainton, Roland Herbert, 1894-
    The medieval church.

    Reprint of the edition published by D. Van Nostrand,
Co., Princeton, N.J., in series: An Anvil original.
    Bibliography: p.
    Includes index.
    1. Church history—Middle Ages, 600-1500.   I. Title.
[BR252.B26   1979]   270   78-11433
ISBN 0-88275-786-5

    10   9   8   7   6   5   4

TABLE OF CONTENTS

PART II—DOCUMENTS

Part I

THE MEDIEVAL CHURCH

— 1 —

MONKS, POPES AND BARBARIANS

A history of the Church in the Middle Ages must of necessity be a history of the Church in the west, because in the east there were no middle ages. The barbarian invasions did not crash the portals of the Dardanelles. The Moslem incursion restricted the territory without disrupting the continuity of the eastern empire. The first crucial break was occasioned by the capture of Constantinople by the Turks in 1453, and that date falls in the period which in the west is usually called the high Renaissance. Of course a history of Christianity which omits the eastern Church is inadequate, but this Anvil book is frankly the history only of a segment, albeit a segment so large as to bulge the seams. The chronological limits are approximately 400 to 1500 A.D.

The period begins with the barbarian invasions in the west. Great difference of opinion exists as to how disruptive they actually were of the culture of the Christian Roman empire. St. Jerome's lament (*see Reading No. 1*) sounds as if the fall of Rome in 410 A.D. marked the end of the ages, but St. Augustine sagely remarked that present fleas are always deemed worse than past fevers, and therefore commissioned his student Orosius to write a history of the world in order to reassure his countrymen, seeing that earlier times had weathered calamities no less grievous.

Historians in our day are disposed to inquire whether later disruptions were not worse than the first. There were three waves of invasion extending over a period of some

six hundred years. First came the inroads of the conti-
nental Germans. When they had subsided, the horn of
the Crescent swung like a comet across northern Africa
to the Pyrenees until arrested in the early eighth century.
When the scimitars of Allah were contained within the
Iberian peninsula, the non-European Germans from the
Scandinavian lands—the Vikings—began in the ninth and
tenth centuries swooping on the islands and raiding up the
rivers to the very gates of Paris. For a time they threatened
to incorporate England into a Scandinavian confederation.
She was realigned with Europe through the conquest by a
scion of earlier Viking invaders of the land named after
them as Normandy. In the meantime Magyars and Slavs
were beating upon Eastern Europe. Until well after the
year 1000 A.D. Europe was in a state of siege.

Those who minimize the impact of the first invasions
point out that they were only the culmination of a long
process of controlled immigration. Nor were the intruders
sufficiently numerous or ruthless to displace the older
population. The Franks in Gaul constituted only some
15% to 20%. The great change lay in the disruption of
universal government. The cultural gap between barbarian
and Roman is said to have been exaggerated. The invaders
were not nomads but land-hungry soil tillers, who—finding land—ceased to kill and began to till. They had long
had contacts with Rome and as craftsmen were not inferior.

The gap can be diminished by showing that the barbarians were as civilized as the Romans, or that the
Romans were as barbarian as the barbarians. They were
all barbarous. When Theodoric conquered Odavaçar he
clave him with a stroke from skull to loin, saying, "The
villain seemed to have no bones." Alboin compelled his
wife to drink from a goblet fashioned from the skull of
her father. But what shall we say of the Romans who constructed amphitheaters for the sport of watching men kill
and die? Salvian testified that the barbarians were more
chaste than the Romans. One wonders. Three hundred
years later Boniface told the Saxons of England and Saxony that by reason of drunkenness and sensuality they
were a stench in the nostrils of the Franks and the Lombards. Accurate comparisons are futile, but this is plain:
Rome never had been really Christianized, and the bar-

barians, whether pagan or Arian Christians, were a lusty lot with no taste for the yoke of the gospel. (The Arians were Christian heretics who subordinated the Son in the Trinity to the Father.)

The Church's Task. The Church faced a formidable task in converting the heathen to Christianity and the heretics to orthodoxy. The task was facilitated by the comparative cultural unity of the Germanic peoples. Despite dialects, they spoke more of a common tongue than the Romans, for Latin in the west had not displaced Basque, Punic and Celtic, nor had Greek in the east supplanted Syrian, Coptic, and Armenian. The Bible of Ulfilas could serve all of the Germanic folk and the Englishman Boniface preached to huge throngs from Frisia to Thuringia apparently without an interpreter. The organization was tribal. The King with his long hair had a sacral character. Crimes of blood could be redeemed in money. Religiously the northerners were in the twilight of the gods, ready to identify their own with those of Rome, Wodin with Mercury, Thor with Jove, and even to adopt outright the religion at the time dominant among the Romans, whether Arianism in the days of Ulfilas, or Nicene orthodoxy after Theodosius.

Certain tenets of Christianity appealed to the barbarians. They could appreciate the Victor over the dark domain of death, but they did not esteem the lowliness of Christ, and the cross required centuries to seize upon the imagination of the west. The pacific tenets of Christianity were unintelligible. Jesus rather was made into a tribal war god; so also were Peter and the archangel Michael. The first Christian poem in the Germanic tongue celebrates the mighty deed of that doughty swordsman Simon Peter, who to shield his Suzerain drew his sharp blade and clave clean the ear of the high priest's servant. Monasticism was incomprehensible. One of the Gauls, hearing that fasting is the food of angels, avowed no aspiration to be in that category. Only one Goth is reported to have been in the monastery of St. Benedict. Presumably the Germans adopted monasticism only after it became an active force in society.

One advantage conferred by the invasions on the church of Rome was greater freedom. The eastern emperors were too remote to interfere and the Arian kings did not try. Theodoric, when in Rome, did reverence at the tombs of the apostles. Councils were free to convene and the popes to direct the churches of their faith. The Arian churches did not, of course, look to orthodox Rome, nor had they a center of their own in Rome. They were decentralized, attached to kings or lay patrons, and after conversion to orthodoxy were not disposed to bow to Rome. Hence, the tension between the centralizing and the decentralizing tendencies which plagued the Middle Ages. Theologically, the barbarians were not interested in the slogans of the old Greek Arianism, except that they tended to subordinate Christ and to make of him only a glorified Viking. Some think this is the reason that Christianity completely disappeared in northern Africa, for a deified chieftain could not withstand the impact of Allah and his prophet. But there is also the possibility that the Berbers and the Punics, long disaffected because of the demolition of Carthage, had their revenge in defection from the faith of Rome.

In the winning of the west three great institutions were at work, sometimes in collaboration, sometimes independently. The three were monasticism, the papacy and the civil state. The first two can be characterized at the outset, but the civil state and its role can better be described in the course of its emergence.

The Role of Monasticism. Monasticism exhibited the form given to it by St. Benedict in the middle of the sixth century. This was the period of Justinian, when Italy was temporarily recovered for the empire. Benedictine monasticism, in other words, did not originate in order to deal with the barbarians. Rather it arose by transfer from the east, but with modifications born of experience and conformable with good sense. The eastern monks in the first flush of their enthusiasm had practiced extravagant asceticisms, macerations of the body, contests in austerity which not infrequently issued in insanity, suicide or a return to the world. Pachomius had already tempered the movement by introducing community living in place of the hermit life, and St. Basil went further by way of codification. St. Benedict, the Roman, had an eye both to earth and to heaven. Of course heaven came first. The great object of monasticism was never to be comfortable, nor even to survive, but to honor God, to enjoy Him and to implore His favor upon the petitioners and their friends in the world. The purpose of monasteries was not to break in new lands, fell forests, drain marshes, educate children or copy manuscripts. All this they did, but only as a by-product of the labor of those who had forsaken the world for the love of God. (*See Reading, No. 1, II B and C.*)

Yet the monks were sufficiently of the world to make themselves independent from the world. After the manner of the world they earned their living with the sweat of their brows and therefore did need to turn to the world for alms, though alms were indeed to come. The Benedictine monastery was self-sufficient, with its own well, fields, mill, orchard, creek, fishpond, sheepstall, cow pasture, rabbitry and barns. The monk need not leave and was forbidden to do so save on urgent business. In that case let two go and, on returning, hold their peace. In addition to the vows of chastity, poverty and obedience was the new vow of stability. No holy tramps allowed! (*See Reading, No. 1, II A.*)

There is a charming tale of how St. Benedict himself was once seduced into spending a night away from his cell. Once a year his custom was to visit his sister Scholastica and spend with her a day in holy converse. On this occasion the day was far spent and the stars appeared. Scholastica begged her brother to stay on through the night. "Sister," he remonstrated, "you know I am not to spend a night away from my cell." At once there blew up such a frightful storm that he could not leave. "What have you done?" he demanded of his sister. "I asked you," said she, "and you would not, so I asked God and He did." Benedict with grace accommodated himself to the Lord's will. On his return he saw in a vision the soul of his sister carried by angels to her heavenly abode, and then he understood.

All of the labor of the monastery was performed by the brothers, whether of the kitchen or of the field. The day was apportioned with no latitude for personal vagaries. The brothers rose at two. The next three hours alternated between prayer and meditation. From five to nine they studied, normally from Christian books, though a pagan book might be issued if the request were made by scratching behind the ear like a dog. From 9:15 to noon the brothers were in the fields. At twelve came the one meal of the day and after it an hour's siesta. Work again out of doors till four. Then compline and bed by 6:30 with some variation for the seasons. Such a life was rugged, liveable and well balanced as to prayer, study and manual labor.

This manner of life was not devised in order to convert the barbarians. At first the Benedictine monasteries were situated as remotely as possible from the barbarians, on mountain promontories perchance, like Monte Cassino looking down on the valley of the Garigliano. Totila the Goth came up to visit Benedict, but barbarians did not make military raids on mountain peaks. Other monasteries were on the islands of the Mediterranean like St. Lerins. The recruits came from the old Roman aristocracy who in a time of turmoil sought tranquility and security. But as the invasions continued, the monasteries came down from the peaks into the vales, and they came in from the isles and went up the rivers and over the mountains. What better instrument could have been devised than these self-sustaining communities to undertake the conversion of the north?

Bear in mind that the papacy could not finance missions. The culture had become agriculture and the economy was largely in kind. There were still some coinage, but a great shortage of small change. How could a missionary have carried a huge pack of denarii over the Alps? How long could he have kept it? And when it was spent how could he have been replenished? The simple fact was that when he crossed the mountains he was on his own. Under these circumstances a group did well to start out together. Among the barbarians they would have no difficulty in securing a tract of unused land on which soon they would be able to take care of themselves.

Then they began to radiate round about, to take in boys for education, to perform the sacraments for their neighbors, which meant of course that the monks had become priests, some of them at least. In time they came to be esteemed and loved for their charity and for their prayers. The nobles desired to be buried near the house where prayer was wont to be said. The affluent delighted to bestow their lands upon those who would use them well and would confer eternal favors upon their benefactors. Nothing in the Rule of St. Benedict forbade the receiving of gifts. The individual monk was to have absolutely nothing, not even his own underwear, but the community was different. Lands were given and lands were received, and with the lands went the workers on the lands, the serfs. What was the monastery to do with them? If they were cast off, where would they go? If they were kept, what would the monks do with themselves? No longer needed for manual labor, they might devote more time to prayer, to teaching, to copying, and they would have to devote some to administration, to direct the serfs. Then if the land produced a superabundance, there would be occasion for selling and buying. This very situation contained the seed of corruption. Caesar of Heisterbach, himself a monk, formulated the law of monasticism in these terms: "Discipline begets abundance, and abundance, unless we take the utmost care, destroys discipline; discipline in its fall pulls down abundance." And the cycle begins again. But to center on decadence is not just. Every great monastic movement has enjoyed several centuries of vitality and then has had to be renewed by another. Our concern here is with the days when the sons of Benedict were taming the barbarians.

The Role of the Papacy. The second great institution was the papacy. It did not initiate all, by any means, of the missionary endeavors. In the early centuries the papacy was not always the center of the Church's vitality. Through many vicissitudes it took on shape and performed a role. What kind of a role nowhere better appears than in the case of the pontificate of Gregory I (590-640 A.D.). He belonged to the period when the empire of Justinian had receded again to the east, and new barbarians, the Lombards, had entered Italy in the north, with some patches also in the south. They were Arians. Gregory called them "the unspeakable Lombards," but primarily because their system of taxation was so light that some of the old Romans were guilty of defection to their suzerainty. But most of the older population feared them greatly because they were guilty of extending their kingdom and particularly of capturing the old Romans and of selling them into slavery unless they were ransomed. Where was the ransom money to be found? The emperor still had an official called the exarch at Ravenna, but he had no money. There was still a pretorian prefect at Rome with a silver inkstand, which would not go far in redeeming captives. The metropolis of Rome itself could supply nothing. Its city of statues was reduced to mutilated marble torsos sprawling over cobblestones. The aqueducts had been cut. The higher regions of the city then became uninhabitable. The lowlands of the Campania had been flooded, and malaria was rife. Refugees poured into Rome. Hitherto the government, since the days of the early empire, had supplied the populace with bread and circuses. Who now would meet these needs? The Church and only the Church, not circuses indeed, but bread and the means of ransom!

The Church had property, amazing amounts of property—wooded lands in Calabria, wheat lands in Africa, other lands on the islands and on the mainland as far north as Istria. Within Italy itself, the pope could command coin as well as kind. For the administration of these vast estates, all ultimately the result of donations, an entire bureaucracy had been developed (*see Reading No. 1, III B*), to whom the pope sent out orders gentle or peremptory. Every letter clicked with a decision. Who commissioned the ships, brought in the grain and fed the people? None other than the bishop of Rome. Let us call him now for convenience the pope. The title was already in use, but was not restricted exclusively to the bishop of Rome prior to the eleventh century. Still, in common parlance, it is employed retroactively with reference to the early centuries. The pope, then, fed the people, the pope redeemed the captives, the pope had dealings with the barbarian Lombards, the pope made treaties. The emperor at Constantinople fulminated. But what could he do or say? He had neither money nor men.

This situation marks really the beginning of the temporal power of the papacy. There was no formal recognition as yet, but in the feeding of the populace and in dealing with the political powers, the pope was performing functions hitherto discharged by the civil state. In all of this there was no grasping after power. Gregory I would vastly have preferred to have been a monk. He was burdened by such a weight of administration. He had simply stepped into an emergency to do what needed to be done and what no one else was in a position to do. The tragedy of the Church and of many another institution is that she finds it hard to step out when her task is done, and some one else is better qualified to take over. But her reluctance to relinquish power should not serve as a reproach for having assumed it in a day of necessity.

Nor should the impression be given that Pope Gregory was utterly preoccupied with administration. His sermons are still classics of Catholic devotion. His *Pastoral Rule* is charged with gracious sagacity. As a theologian he was not a decisive figure, but he is credited with having first formulated the doctrine of purgatory—and what doctrine more than this shaped the piety of the Middle Ages? (*See Reading No. 1, III A and C.*)

— 2 —

CONVERSION OF THE EUROPEAN HEARTLAND

By the time of the first barbarian inroads, the Roman empire was ostensibly and prevailingly Christian from the Euphrates to the Clyde. To be sure, pagans there were still, and their taunts that the invasions were due to the anger of their gods against Christianity goaded St. Augustine to compose his great reply. But broadly speaking, one may talk of the Christian Roman empire. And the barbarians, too, as already noted, were not untouched. The Vandals, Ostrogoths, Visigoths, Burgundians and Lombards were Arian Christians; the Suevi, Franks, Angles, Saxons, Jutes—and, of course, the Huns—were pagan. The Church was confronted with the formidable task of making the heretics orthodox and the pagans Christian. The process took well nigh a thousand years until the most northerly regions had been encompassed. Very roughly, one can block out the stages by lands, centuries and persons. In the early fifth century we have the conversion of Ireland through Patrick; at the end of that century, the conversion of the Franks under Clovis. A hundred years later, at the end of the sixth century, Reccared brought the Visigoths of Spain to orthodoxy. Almost coincidentally, Augustine of Canterbury set out for the British Isles. In the eighth century Boniface was active in Germany. In the ninth, Ansgar worked with the Danes, and Cyril and Methodius with the southern Slavs. In the late tenth century the two Olafs converted Norway, and at the same time Vladimir introduced Christianity into southern Russia. To give the impression that so vast a work was accomplished by so few would be manifestly false. A scant dozen missionaries have acquired a real or legendary prominence, but the conversion of Europe was achieved by a host of the unrecorded.

Ireland. The work went on undeterred by continuing waves of invasion—and in part because of them. More than once, some raiding rover was captured by the faith of those he pillaged and took it back to his own land. Then again, a captive might become a missionary. This happened in Ireland. When the Roman legions were withdrawn from the British Isles for the defense of the continent, the Scots from Ireland (the Irish then were Scots) raided the west coast of England and carried off Patrick. From his own pen we have an account of his captivity, escape and voluntary return in response to a vision. (*See Reading No. 2, I.*) Unfortunately, his story ends where we would like to have had it begin. From other sources we know that he went back to the continent for preliminary training and was there detained fourteen years because of his *rusticitas*. In the end he was commissioned as a bishop by the pope. From then on we have but legends. One in particular enshrines several truths. The story is that an Irish chieftain presented Patrick with a bronze cauldron. Patrick said *Gratzacham* (a corruption of *gratiam agimus,* we thank you). The chieftain learning that this was his only response ordered that it be taken away from him. Again Patrick said *Gratzacham*. The chieftain, astounded that he should give thanks for a loss as well as for a gain, ordered that it be restored and that a piece of land be added. From this tale we learn that Patrick dealt with the head of a tribal organization. The missionaries commonly made their initial approach through the ruler. Without at least his benevolent neutrality, they could make little headway. Secondly, they acquired land, and thereby the Church came to be geared into the entire social structure of an agrarian society.

In these two respects Patrick was accommodating himself to Ireland. But the use of Latin meant that he was European and that he was for the first time bringing Ireland within the pale of the classical Christian civilization. Not the legions, but the missionaries, made Ireland a constituent of the empire; Ireland then in turn was to assist Europe in preserving her own tradition. South of the Rhine, Latin was in danger of disappearing through transformation into the vernaculars then taking shape. There was no danger of this in Ireland where the vernacular was Gaelic. Latin was for the Irish the language of the Church and of the scholar. Therefore it remained the better intact and from Ireland was to be brought back to the continent, there to serve as a *lingua franca* among the Spaniards, the French and the Italians (who, in their modifications of Latin, were becoming unintelligible to each other).

Another point to be noted is that Christianity entered Ireland through seculars and after a century was in the hands of regulars. These are technical terms used to describe two branches of the ministry. "Secular" has reference to the Church in the world (*saeculum*) rather than in the monastery. The whole hierarchy of the parish clergy —priests, bishops, archbishops, metropolitans and the pope himself—are seculars. The monks were called "regulars" because they followed the rule (*regula*). But the distinction is not absolute. Some cathedrals were staffed by regulars. Some half dozen in England were Benedictine, and conversely a monastery might undertake pastoral functions to the region round about, as in Ireland.

A further contribution of Ireland to the continent was the development of a system of private penance whereby the offender confessed not publicly before the congregation, but in secret to the priest. Manuals called penitentials were composed for the guidance of confessors. One wonders sometimes whether the questions he was instructed to ask might not have put ideas into the minds of his flock. But then one recalls that they were a rough crew who needed no hints as to sexual irregularities or plain murder. The common practice was to baptize by masses. The advantage of this practice was that the convert was not dissociated from his ethnic group, the disadvantage that he carried over into his Christianity a large measure of his pagan faith and mores. Such conversion meant little more than that the way was now open for genuine Christianizing.

Gaul. This was notably true in Gaul, where the pagan Franks embraced the faith *en masse* at the behest of King Clovis. (*See Reading No. 2, II.*) The reasons for his own conversion have been variously assessed. The classical account, on the face of it, indicates that he believed Jesus to be the god who had given him a victory. He may have believed just that, but had he calculated he would have observed that the neighboring states were Arian and for him to embrace orthodox Christianity might be productive of friction. But since he wanted to conquer them anyway, friction might not have been unwelcome. And since the old Roman population was everywhere the majority and was orthodox, his sway at home might be easier to defend and abroad easier to extend if his faith were that of the masses. At any rate so it proved.

But the quality of the faith affords a glaring example of the observation just made with reference to Ireland. After the conversion of Clovis, Gregory, the bishop of Tours, records murders in the cathedrals with churchmen as assassins, and he says he might have told worse had he not feared to be thought to speak ill of his brethren. On reading his pages, one is appalled by the magnitude of the task undertaken by the Church in taming these undisciplined hordes.

One consequence of the conversion of Clovis to orthodoxy went at the time quite unnoticed, but was destined to be of great consequence. Gaul was thereby oriented toward Rome. This was a full century before the Visigoths and the Lombards became orthodox. When the popes were in need of help from the civil power, it was in consequence to the Franks that they turned. To be sure, the Lombards may have been too close to be convenient allies, and the Visigoths in Spain too remote. Yet the earlier alignment with Gaul may explain why the Merovingians and the Carolingians were to be the pope's great allies.

Another not insignificant result of the conversion of Clovis was that Gaul could become a highroad between

Rome and the British Isles, and between them and the whole of the continent. The Irish early became missionary. Columba in 563 A.D. went to Scotland and planted a monastery at Iona. Columbanus early in the next century came back to the continent. He might not have had free access had the king of the Franks been Arian. Columbanus did not come exactly as a missionary, but rather because the Irish monastic discipline esteemed as an ascetic exercise that one should live and die in a strange land. But Columbanus was a missionary for Irish monasticism. In France he founded the monastery of Luxeuil and in Italy that of Bobbio. His disciple St. Gall established the monastery in Switzerland which bears his name.

At the same time, missionaries sent out from Rome were able to traverse Gaul on their way to England, as in the case of Augustine of Canterbury (always so denominated to distinguish him from Augustine of Hippo). His success was due to a situation oft recurring whereby an Orthodox Christian queen from the older population brought her barbarian husband either to the faith or to an attitude of tolerance. Ethelbert of Kent was married to a princess from the continent, Bertha, and she plied her gentle suasion with unremitting importunity. This was a repetition of the case of Clothilde and Clovis. Similarly among the Lombards, Theodolinda won Agilulf and in Northumbria the daughter of Bertha and Ethelbert converted her husband. The domestic aspect of these conversions should not, however, be overplayed. The real point was that the barbarian king admired the culture of the conquered. He valued a political alliance which would enhance his favor with the older populance and link him with a more established kingdom. These examples display the process whereby the invader became accommodated to the invaded. (*See Reading No. 2, III A.*)

England. The mission of Augustine, who with royal consent founded the see of Canterbury, spread until contacts were made with the older Christian inhabitants of Britain, the Celts, who had been driven to the west coast into Cornwall, Wales and Lancashire. Moreover, the missions started by the Irish in Scotland had become expansive and were working down from the north into England. The prominent figure was Aidan. When contacts were made between the Celtic and the Roman

Christians, differences of practice became apparent. The basic difference was, of course, that the Celts had been so long largely isolated from the continent that they had not been in touch with the developments which centered at Rome. Two discrepancies attracted attention. One was the form of the tonsure. The Romans shaved the top of the head and left a rim of hair above the ears in memory of the crown of thorns. The Celts shaved right up to a tuft on the crown, presumably after the manner of the Druid priests. Another difference had to do with the celebration of Easter. This was called the Quartodeciman controversy, harking back to the old dispute whether Jesus died on the fourteenth or fifteenth of the month Nisan. That point had long since been forgotten. The discrepancy now concerned the calculation of the incidence of Easter, because Rome in the meantime had been able to work out more accurate tables. The upshot of it was that the Celts might be feasting following Easter while the Saxons were fasting during Holy Week. The very household of King Oswy was divided. He was another of those kings with an imported wife. She looked to the south, to Rome whence her Christianity had come; he to the north, to the Celts in the tradition of St. Columba. At a conference held at Whitby in 664 A.D. (*see Reading No. 2, III B*), the king was persuaded to align himself with the Roman practice. The British Isles were soon thereafter reintegrated with the continent and with Rome.

Germany.   The conversion, or at any rate the Christian organization of Germany, was a result of this new orientation. The great missionary to Germany was a Saxon called Winifred, the lover of peace, who, when commissioned as a bishop and a missionary by the pope, received the name of Boniface, the doer of good. His first mission was in Frisia. Later he worked in Hesse, Thuringia and Bavaria. The pope made him the Archbishop of Mainz. He founded the monastery at Fulda. Thus he combined in his own person the secular and the regular forms of the ministry. In many other respects he was an integrating figure. He brought England and France into conjunction, then France and Germany, and strove to bring all into subordination to Rome. Witness his commission from the pope and his oath of allegiance to the pope. (*See Reading No. 2, IV A and B.*)

But of all his achievements, none was perchance of greater significance than the alliance which he helped to cement between the papacy and the kingdom of the Franks. We must bear in mind that the church in Gaul was already very intimately geared into the social fabric and closely allied with the monarchy. We have already observed that the Church, in order to operate, had to become landed. Her success in Gaul had been so great that she had come to control one-quarter to one-third of the land in the realm. This would include lands held by the seculars and by the regulars. Abbots and bishops were vested with this property on behalf of the Church, which no longer held lands as a corporation as in the days of the empire. The church officials were in consequence all the more in a position comparable to that of the lay lords to whom the king turned for levies and military contingents. The bishop and even the abbot would head his own troops despite the prohibition of the Church of the shedding of blood. One bishop got around that by killing nine men with a club instead of an axe so that no blood was shed. The prince bishop had emerged. The incompatibility of the roles did not escape attention. A peasant gaping at the equipage of a prince bishop and being asked why he stared, said that he had not expected to see a bishop so accoutered. The retort was that the display applied only to the role of the prince. "But, suppose," countered the peasant, "the devil should take the prince to hell, what would become of the bishop?" Not infrequently, the king found that the services voluntarily rendered by these ecclesiastics did not suffice. Then he would expropriate their lands and bestow them on lay lords who had rendered ampler service. Charles Martel was notorious at this point. Legend had it that when he was buried in St. Denis, the devil slipped in ahead of the saint and took his soul to hell. A later monarch, no less disposed to despoil the Church, but resolved to avoid this fate, had himself buried in another church whose saint could be trusted to be more on the alert than St. Denis. But actually the Church did not greatly suffer, because new donations compensated for deprivations. The proportion

of the Church's holdings remained about the same. The
king's control was exercised mainly through the appointments of abbots and bishops who must be amenable to
his will. What all of this added up to was a very close
association of Church, state and society with a tendency
to decentralization of the Church universal.

— 3 —

THE CHURCH AND
THE KINGDOM OF
THE FRANKS

But a special circumstance arose which made the papacy indispensable to the Carolingians. The founders of
this house were not the monarchs of France, but were
known as the mayors of the palace. The decadent Merovingians with their long hair, the symbol of the sacral
character of kingship, were required to give the sanction
of regality to decisions made by their more energetic ad-
ministrators. Pippin, Mayor of the Palace, inquired of
the pope whether it were not appropriate that actual
power and the title of king should be conjoined. This was
more than a hint at a coronation at the hands of the
Church. The idea may well have come from Boniface.
The Saxons practiced such rites as a recognition of the
divine origin of kingship. The king was not a god, and he
was not a priest, but he was more than an ordinary layman. A certain divine afflatus hovered above his brow.
To this the ceremony of coronation bore token.

Now the pope had good reason for acceding to the
hint because he also had his needs. Despite the fact that
Gregory I and his successors had used the wealth of the
Church to perform some functions hitherto exercised by
the state, the papacy was not actually a civil state and,

in particular, had no armed forces at her disposal. Her security was menaced on several counts, first by the populace of Rome. The popes of Rome had their most persistent annoyance from the people of Rome. Naturally, if the papacy were wealthy and influential, the great Roman families wanted to fill the position of pope with one of their scions. A papal election was often signalized by a riot. Then there were the Lombards. Gregory I had bought them off and no doubt restrained them in a measure through his influence with their orthodox queen. Yet they did not cease their depradations.

But worst of all was Constantinople. The eastern emperors still claimed jurisdiction over Italy, and on occasion they had been able to make good the claim. Justinian in the middle of the sixth century had recovered the peninsula. He then sought to compel the pope to support his ecclesiastical policy of conciliating the Monophysite heretics in the East, who held that Christ had only one divine nature. Pope Vigilius was uncooperative. The emperor deported him to Constantinople. Intimidated, the pope (who happened to have a beard) fled to an altar. Imperial emissaries tugged at his beard. The beard held, the altar collapsed, the pope capitulated. Worse was the fate of Martin I, who was quite truculent in opposition to the emperor's attempts to placate the Monophysites by conceding that Christ had only one divine will. This position was called Monothelite. When Martin would not comply, he also was deported to Constantinople and so maltreated that he died. The popes naturally wished to be free from all such intimidations. Pope Gelasius I, even before Justinian, had sought to define the relations of the Church and the empire by his famous demarcation of the two spheres of jurisdiction. (*See Reading No. 3, I.*) There is, said he, a royal power and a sacred authority. Each should conduct its own administration, but rulers should remember that the sphere of the secular is vastly inferior to the sphere of the sacred.

Early in the eighth century, Gregory II had indulged in blithe defiance of the eastern emperor. (*See Reading No. 3, II.*) The controversy this time had to do with the use of holy images: the crucifix, and statues or paintings of the Mother of God and the saints. Leo III, called the Isaurian, issued an order for their destruction, but when

some of his men mounted a ladder to take down a crucifix over a gate in Constantinople, a crowd of women
pulled the ladder from under them and beat them to
death. The motives of Leo are not entirely clear. Some
think that he was an enlightened rationalist, who objected
to such superstitions as that an image of the Virgin
down a well would keep it from going dry. Others claim
that he sought to exalt the state by removing all religious
symbolism from the coins. Others again sense an influence of Mohammedanism, which refused to represent the
human figure. Very probably, iconoclasm was connected
with the view of the Monophysites that Christ did not
have a human nature at all, and to portray the divine nature would be idolatry. (*See Reading No. 3, III.*) Further, it was argued that images were condemned in the
ten commandments. The supporters of the images appealed to the doctrine of the incarnation. God Himself in
Christ became flesh. In that case the material cannot be
evil. Similarly, Christ's body is present in the physical
elements on the altar. Why then may it not be represented pictorially? The upshot in the East was the restoration of the images, with this limitation: only painting
and bas-relief were allowed. The test was whether the
thumb and finger could be made to hold on the nose of
the image. The West consistently defended the images,
and if a council under Charlemagne dissented from the
decision of the seventh ecumenical council which restored
the images in the East (785 A.D.), the reason was only
that the decree was incorrectly translated. But the point
for the moment is that Pope Gregory II was in vehement
conflict with Leo III and very contemptuous of his threats,
since actually he controlled an area not more than three
miles around Rome.

The Coronation of Pippin. Perhaps so at the moment, but so much bluster betrayed uneasiness. Might not
another emperor like Justinian restore control over Italy?
Would not the popes be more secure with regard to the
eastern emperor and with regard to the Roman populace
and the Lombards if there were some other political
power on which to rely in the West? We do not know
whether the pope was thinking of all this when Pippin
inquired whether power and title might not be conjoined

in France. At any rate the pope agreed. The common assumption is that Boniface performed the rite of coronation, which was later reenacted by Pope Stephen II. The Church thus presided over the birth of the Carolingian empire. The coronation did not mean that the Church had actually conferred kingship, though this was to be a later interpretation. The Church had essentially witnessed to a transfer of the sacral kingship from the decadent to those who by their actual exercise of power plainly enjoyed the mandate of heaven.

Then in 754 A.D. Pippin performed his part of the tacit covenant. He came to Italy, rapped the knuckles of the Lombards and formally conferred upon the pope rulership over a strip of territory running from Rome over the crest of the Apennines to Ravenna. This territory included five cities, hence called the Pentapolis, whose keys were reverently laid on the tomb of St. Peter. This symbolic act is called the Donation of Pippin. Actually, it did not mark a great change. The popes, as we have seen, had long exercised a measure of jurisdiction, and they were not now equipped with troops. If military support were necessary, it would still have to come from the kingdom of the Franks.

At about this same time originated another donation, a document called the *Donation of Constantine,* spurious but highly influential. The claim was that Constantine, out of gratitude for having been cured of the leprosy, announced that as emperor he would not becloud the eminence of the successor of St. Peter by residing in the same city and would therefore withdraw to Constantinople, leaving to the pope temporal jurisdiction over the whole of the West. (*See Reading No. 3, IV.*) No great perspicacity ought to have been needed to prove that the popes never had enjoyed such jurisdiction. Yet it was not until the time of the Renaissance that the forgery was demonstrated by Cusa and Valla. Those who in the Middle Ages dissented from the doctrine of the universal temporal power of the popes did not impugn the authenticity of the document, but simply said that Constantine had had no business to make the pope into a civil ruler. One may doubt whether really the forger desired so much. His main concern was to emancipate the popes from subservience to the emperors in the East. That could best be done by an alliance with the kingdom of the Franks.

The Coronation of Charlemagne. This development came to a more striking fruition in the case of Pippin's son Charles, known as Charlemagne. He established an empire greater in extent than any since the days of imperial Rome, and greater than any since, unless the sway of Innocent III be called an empire. Charlemagne had under his tutelage the east to the confines of Bulgaria, the south to somewhat beyond the Pyrenees, the north extending into Saxony and the west to the ocean. He was remarkable in his ability to marshal military forces and to strike swiftly and surely. He considered himself a *Christianissimus rex*. Einhard, his biographer, said that he daily attended church when his health permitted, and he was not frail. He kept his finger on ecclesiastical appointments, doubly so because he relied on the clergy to supply him with a corps of educated officials. He was interested in the liturgy and himself attended choir practice. About him he gathered a brilliant coterie of Christian scholars, English, German and Italian. Charlemagne himself spoke German and struggled only with labor to acquire Latin, but he desired that his scholars should keep alive the ancient culture. The art of illumination reached a high eminence in the Carolingian school. Charlemagne believed himself divinely commissioned to spread the faith and converted the Saxons in 26 campaigns, finally inflicting the death penalty upon those who refused baptism. Against such violence, though even more against the levying of tithes on forced converts, Alcuin raised his voice in protest. (*See Reading 2, IV C and D.*)

The relations already established with the papacy by Pippin reached their culmination under Charlemagne. The initiative appears to have come from the papacy. Leo III was being shamefully treated by the Roman populace, and the Lombards were not lamblike. The pope appealed to Charlemagne, who made an incursion into Italy, vindicating the reputation of the pope and ending the kingdom of the Lombards. Then on Christmas day, as Charles was kneeling in the basilica of St. Peter, the pope stole up behind him and placed a crown upon his head, hailing him as the Emperor of the Romans.

Some have supposed that this scene had been planned and even rehearsed by both parties, but Einhard declared that his master would never have gone into the church that day had he known what was going to happen. The manner in which he modified the title conferred upon him would indicate that this was true. The biography of Pope Leo says that his words were these: "Life and victory to Charles Augustus, crowned by God, great and pacific emperor of the Romans." (*See Reading No. 3, V.*) Charles styled himself in his documents not as "the emperor of the Romans," but as "the one who governs the Roman realm." Einhard says that he finally accepted the titles of augustus and emperor, but with the omission of the expression "of the Romans." One must remember that the Byzantines were still calling themselves the Romans in the days of the crusades. Charlemagne would seem to have wished an arrangement like that set up by Diocletian with two *augusti,* one for the east and one for the west. There was no desire to affront the Byzantine *basileus,* nor, as some contemporaries alleged, to transfer the empire from the east to the west. The pope's main desire was that he should not be subject to the humiliations visited upon any insubordinate patriarch of Constantinople.

The coronation of Charlemagne gathered up a number of strands which had come even more clearly to light in the liturgies of coronation. (*See Reading No. 3, VII.*) There was the old Germanic concept of sacral kingship to which recognition was given by the Church through anointing with chrism. A parallel was found in the Old Testament in the anointing by Samuel of Saul and David. Alcuin was fond of referring to Charlemagne as David. The crown went back to the days of pagan Rome when the projections of the crown indicated the rays of the sungod. The sceptre used in later coronations came from Rome. The rod was a remnant of the lance of the Teutonic warrior. There was as yet nothing which distinctly declared that the Church was the bestower of kingship or that she was empowered both to make and to unmake. That was to come later.

Dionysius the Areopagite. However, in the period shortly after Charlemagne, a document reached the west which was to have great influence on political as well as

religious thinking. The writings of Dionysius the Areopagite, a Syrian monk of the sixth century, were in Greek.
This Dionysius was erroneously identified with the Dionysius of Mars Hill (Areopagus) mentioned in the seven-
teenth chapter of the book of Acts. And then again he
was identified with the patron saint of France, St. Denis,
the French form of Dionysius; according to legend, after
decapitation he picked up his head and walked a mile. A
wag pertinently remarked that in such cases it is the first
step which counts. The writings ascribed to France's
patron saint actually enshrined a slightly Christianized
Neoplatonic mysticism. The doctrine of the summit of
darkness, the cloud of unknowing, deeply affected western mysticism of the negative way. With regard to the relations of Church and state, the influential writings were
two, *The Celestial* and the *Terrestrial Hierarchies*. (*See
Reading No. 3, VI.*) Each was divided into nine parts,
and each of these subdivided into three. The celestial hierarchy is composed of beings named in the New Testament—angels, archangels, principalities and powers—
but they function more as the emanations of the Gnostic
pleroma. The terrestrial hierarchy includes the sacraments,
the clergy and the laity, each subdivided into three. The
core is the Neoplatonic concept of the ultimate One, the
ineffable superessential intelligence which communicates
its being by way of illumination through descending
grades of the celestial to the terrestrial hierarchy, and
thence is transmitted through the sacraments by the clergy
to the laity. The function of the priest is to lead the laity
in contemplation until, rapt by the glory of the thearchic
splendor, they are united to the being of the Ultimate
One. Important throughout is the hierarchical idea. The
clergy are above the laity and the higher clergy above the
lower. Their especial preeminence lies in this: that they
are the hierophants on the ladder of ascent. By this philosophy the hierarchic structure of the Church and of
society received a grounding in the very fabric of the
cosmos. This work was translated into Latin by an Irish-
man, Scotus Erigena, Scotus the Erin born, in the period
just following Charlemagne, and provided a basis for later
claims by the Church.

— 4 —

THE TWO SWORDS

The two centuries following Charlemagne, the ninth and the tenth, are often called dark, though historians of late have been discovering some glimmers of light. Some suggest that the greatest gain was a very slight economic revolution in the north in the substitution of third- instead of second-year fallowing. This was possible in the north because of the abundant rainfall. And the increased yield made possible the introduction of horse rather than ox power. This unrecorded transformation was taking place on many a peasant holding, even while the Vikings were swooping over fields and meadows and carrying off produce and men. But disorder there certainly was, and if institutions declined and literature languished, we should rather be amazed that anything survived. Most astounding is what happened to the raiders. The Vikings, whose beaked prows in the ninth century invested a moonlit night with terror, by the end of the tenth were pruning apple orchards in Normandy.

After Charlemagne the empire rather than the Church declined, partly because of the interminable raids, partly because the Teutonic system of the divided inheritance triumphed over the Roman principle of a single succession. The culmination of the process was the division at Verdun in 843 A.D. which created Germany and France and a middle strip running down the left bank of the Rhine, along the Rhone and through Italy. This area, being assigned to Lothair, was called *Lothari regnum,* whence the name Lorraine.

During this period of political disintegration there was a great pope, Nicholas I. His pontificate was marked by three controversies. One was with Constantinople directed

29

against the patriarch Photius, and hence called the Photian schism. The issues were trivial. The breach between the eastern and the western churches did not become definitive until 1054 A.D. But it was never absolute, and yet for a long time had been relatively actual.

The other two controversies were in the west. One was with Hinçmar, the archbishop of Rheims and metropolitan of France, who denied to a priest, whom he had disciplined, the right of appeal to Rome. This was an assertion of the local autonomy of the Frankish church, whereas the pope was affirming the universal jurisdiction of the centralized church. About this time there appeared in France a body of material known as the Pseudo-Isidorian Decretals, a collection of many genuine papal decretals interspersed with forgeries which asserted that from the beginning the Church of Rome had exercised authority over the other churches. The claim was made that the clergy should not be subject to the civil courts, that any priest might appeal to Rome. The proposal was made that a college of churchmen should be formed beneath the pope but above any metropolitan, an idea later implemented in the college of cardinals. The interesting point is that these claims did not emanate from the pope, and we are not altogether sure whether Nicholas knew of them. The lower clergy in France put forward these claims in order to protect themselves against the higher clergy in their own region. The drive for centralization came from the bottom as a safeguard against the middle. These pretensions were, of course, not realized at this time, but the documents survived to serve as a warrant for subsequent claims. The third controversy was with Lothair, the ruler of that middle strip, who had put away his wife and taken a concubine. The pope ordered him to return to his spouse, and in the end the king capitulated. The weapon used against him was excommunication. That exclusion from the sacraments could bring a king to compliance is something to ponder. By what stages had such influence been acquired? To be sure, four centuries had elapsed between the conversion of Clovis and the pontificate of Nicholas. But during this interval we know so little about the way in which the people were trained from parish to parish that we are bound to be startled when the veil lifts and we see what measure of success had been achieved.

The people had really come to believe that their eternal salvation depended on the rites of the Church, and, even if the king did not believe it, he could not disregard the faith of his people. One begins to understand why the pope after all did not need armies. He had a more potent weapon than the sword.

Northward Expansion. During this period the expansion of Christianity was continuing. Harald of Denmark, expelled from his kingdom, sought help from the king of France and was told that this would be the more readily forthcoming if he were a Christian. (*See Reading No. 2, V.*) This not too veiled hint disposed him to baptism and even to the introduction of a missionary into his lands. The man was Ansgar. At the same time the gospel was carried to the Slavs in Bulgaria and Moravia by Cyril (baptized Constantine) and Methodius. (*See Reading No. 2, VI.*) An alphabet was devised for the Slavic tongue, and the Bible translated. The liturgy rendered into Slavic became basic for all of the Slavic countries even after the differentation of the Slavic tongues. Bulgaria has always been in a dubious position ecclesiastically between Constantinople, from whom independence was desired, and Rome, from whom interference was not relished. Alliances now with one, now with the other, have alternated with independence. Under Nicholas I there was a temporary recognition of Rome. Moravia, out of enmity for the Roman Catholic Germans, has leaned to Constantinople.

In the late tenth century Christianity was introduced into Norway by the two Olafs, not without violence in their own domains. Charlemagne was the only one to apply constraint to convert another people beyond his jurisdiction. But Olaf Trygvason was not above the massacre of recalcitrant pagan nobles. (*See Reading No. 2, VII.*)

At about the same time Vladimir embraced Christianity and introduced it into southern Russia with the capitol at Kiev. (*See Reading No. 2, VIII.*) Russian Christianity was the daughter of the Byzantine, but with a number of significant differences. Caesaropapism could not in the early centuries be taken over because Russia had no Caesar and no empire. The clergy, as the only learned class, were rather the mentors and educators of the rulers. Another difference was that the Russians did not share the Greek passion for theological speculation. Further,

the Byzantine Church was willing to allow the Slavic
liturgy. Later, when the monarchy developed in Russia,
her church became independent of the Greek, while at
the same time reproducing more nearly the Greek pattern
of Caesaropapism, with the Czar overshadowing and
finally eliminating the patriarch.

After this brief survey of the approximate conversion
of Europe we may reflect on the motifs in the missionary
appeal. Unfortunately, our data as to missionary sermons
are scant. From the fragments one would judge that the
stress was placed on the Christian assurance of a blessed
immortality. One recalls the famous story in the history of
Bede about the Saxon king who compared the life of
man to the flight of a swallow through the banqueting hall
from the darkness into the dark. Paulinus the missionary
informed him that the Christian religion throws light on
the dark beyond. One recalls again that Oswy accepted
the authority of Rome because St. Peter could exclude
him from heaven. (*See Reading No. 2, III B.*) There is a
legend that Methodius terrified Boris of Bulgaria by
painting for him a picture of the judgment day. The resurrection of Christ appears to have been more potent than
the crucifixion, which only much later became central for
the piety of the west. Miracle-working relics appear to
have been a part of the missionary's apparatus. The pagans
were called upon to renounce idols, witchcraft, murder
and sexual irregularities. In a word, one may say that
Christianity was presented as a religion which coupled
ethical demands with the assurance of blessedness on
earth and in heaven.

But to return, the early tenth century was perhaps the
lowest in all Church history with reference to the papacy.
It is called the pornographic period because the popes
were the appointees of prostitutes. How such a situation
could ever have arisen appears utterly incredible, but it
is not so preposterous if one examines the local situation.
The papacy had acquired wealth and influence. The
Roman families wished, therefore, to control the papacy.
The empire of Charlemagne, which might have intervened
to protect the popes against the Romans, had been divided
into three, and its components were ravaged by raids. The
Roman nobility were under the influence of a prostitute,
Marozia, and she waved the baton. The most notorious of

these popes were all named John—John XI, John XII
and John XIII. They may not have been worse than some
of the popes of the Renaissance, but they did not even
compensate for their misdemeanors by elegance.

Cluny Movement. At the same time a great reform
movement was under way, the Cluny movement, an attempt to repristinate early Benedictine monasticism. The
founder was a lay patron, Duke William of Aquitaine,
together with his wife Ingelborga. (*See Reading No. 4, I.*)
He was determined that this monastery was not to be cor-
rupted by interference from anybody, not by his successors as patrons, not by the king and not even by the pope.
Cluny should enjoy freedom to be good. The Cluniacs
were meant to say their prayers. Every one believed that
the prayers of the Cluniacs were exceeding efficacious.
The story is told that Pope Benedict VIII was quite sur-
prised to wake up in hell. He appeared in a vision to a
friend and asked him to implore Odilo of Cluny to pray
for him. Odilo complied, and Benedict in another vision
reported his release.

The Cluniacs were not sequestered from the world,
and in this regard they did not follow too rigidly the rule.
The great of the land frequented their corridors. Odilo,
the abbot, was received in every court as a prince and
with such a company of the brethren that he appeared less
as a prince than as an archangel of monks. The queen
touched his vile garment and shed copious tears. The
unique feature of Cluny was that it founded daughter
houses and retained over them a measure of control, thus
introducing centralization into monasticism. Cluny aimed
first of all at the reform of the monastic life. But Cluny
had an eye also to the reform of lay life and sponsored
the Truce of God and the Peace of God designed to allay
feudal warfare. (*See Reading No. 4, II.*) Cluny sought,
furthermore, the reform of the clergy, an end to the buying of ecclesiastical offices. This was called simony, from
Simon Magus, who tried to buy the Holy Spirit from St.
Peter. The clergy also should give up their wives and be
celibate like the monks. Yet Cluny did not make a great
campaign on these latter points. There was enough to do
to reform the monasteries.

In all of this, Cluny had no objection to lay assistance.
If a godly patron like William of Aquitaine founded a

monastery, why should not a successor equally godly have
something to say as to who should be the abbot? If a
prince, a king or an emperor were genuinely concerned
for the reform of the Church, why should not he—as a
Christian layman in a Christian society and by virtue of
the sacral authority of kingship—intervene to remove the
unworthy and elevate the good?

There were rulers who thought so, notably the Germans
who reconstituted the empire, to be called later the Holy
Roman Empire. There was Otto I, who had himself
crowned by John XII and then displaced the disreputable
pontiff and replaced him by a worthier representative of
St. Peter. And especially there was Otto III, who around
the year 1000 A.D. aspired to restore the glories of ancient
Rome and the purity of the primitive Church. He appointed as pope the most learned man of his day, so
learned that he was suspected of being in league with
Satan. He took the title Sylvester II in memory of that
pope who was alleged to have baptized Constantine and
to have received from him the Donation. Then came another period in which the Italian counts took over. This
was terminated by another intervention by another German emperor, Henry III, a most ardent reformer. The
papacy had come to such a pass that one pope sold the
office, another bought it intending to reform, and a third
was elected by the populace. The emperor swept them all
out and put in a succession of worthy men. The papacy
itself recognized his right to do so. (*See Reading No. 4,
IV C.*) Then Henry died, leaving his widow Agnes in
charge of their infant son, the future Henry IV. One
wonders what would have happened if Henry III had
lived longer and had maintained his strict control. The
interregnum which followed afforded an opportunity to a
group of churchmen committed to a drastic reform.

The Gregorian Reform.   The Gregorian reform is
the name applied to their program, called after Gregory
VII, whose family name was Hildebrand. Others associated with him were Peter Damian and Cardinal Humbert.
They envisioned a genuine revolution. Some of their reforms were those of Cluny. The point of difference was
that the state should have none of the initiative. The
Church could really be pure only if she were independent.
If there was one devout emperor like Henry III, how

many were sons of Belial? The clergy must not only not buy offices. They must not even receive offices as a gift from the lay power. The clergy must no longer be an hereditary dynasty. Clerical celibacy would take care of that. But even more, the Church should become the directive agency even in civil affairs. (*See Reading No. 4, IV.*) Power was claimed for the Church to make and unmake kings. The Church might call upon civil rulers to place their military resources at her disposal, and the pope might even himself lead troops. Leo IX had done so to repulse the Normans in southern Italy. Truly, it might be said that the Church was launching out into the deep.

When Henry IV became of age, the clash came. The pope forbade any lay appointments and dissolved all clerical marriages. Henry defied the pope by making an appointment to the bishopric of Milan. The German clergy defied the pope on the point of marriage and foreswore obedience. The emperor accused the pope of innovation, and there was no doubt about it. Henry IV was proposing to do no more than his father had done with the authorization of a council and a pope. Peter Damian admitted and justified the innovation. Pope Gregory VII, however, insisted that he was only returning to an earlier purity before corruption had set in. There was another point at which he was accused of innovation and utter perversion: that was in claiming for the Church the exercise of the sword. The pope replied by not only excommunicating, but also deposing, the emperor. There followed the famous scene in which the emperor, in order to remove the excommunication, stood as a suppliant for three days in the snow in the courtyard of the fortress at Canossa in January, 1077 A.D., until that "holy demon" of a pontiff released the emperor from the bonds of anathema.

Once again, one cannot but be amazed that the pope's curse could be so effective as even to undercut an emperor's political authority. Once the curse was removed, subjects returned to their allegiance. Then the emperor became defiant and would not take orders from the pope. He was excommunicated again, but this time he marched on Rome with an army, boxed the pope up in the Castello di Sant Angello and set up a counterpope, as his father had done before him. The Normans, who in the meantime had become the pope's allies, rescued him. With them he withdrew to die, saying, "I have loved justice and hated iniquity. Therefore I die in exile." This time the reason for amazement is that the second excommunication did not work. After all, medieval Christians must have had a certain sense of balance. There were two swords, two lights, two authorities. The spiritual was superior to the temporal, but the temporal had also its appointed sphere. If the pope overstepped the bounds, he was not entitled to supine obedience.

The controversy continued. Pope Paschal II proposed to solve it by having the Church give up all her benefices. Let the emperor take over. But nobody wanted that. The bishops certainly did not, and the emperor did not want to get rid of the bishops, but only to control them. The suggestion was dropped. The outcome was a compromise at Worms in 1122 A.D. according to which the election to an ecclesiastical post was to be strictly in the hands of the Church. A bishop was not to receive his office as an investiture from the civil power, but, having been first elected and consecrated, should then swear fealty to the civil ruler. Whether the state, however, by this arrangement lost all control over elections is doubtful. It was not too difficult to suggest to a chapter whom they should elect.

The controversy took place only with the German emperors. In France the local church was on the side of the pope, and the kings did not make a struggle. But the Norman kings in Normandy flatly asserted that the two keys were in the hands of the king and all appointments should emanate from the crown. Gregory VII was too busy fighting the emperor to quarrel with the Normans, especially because other Normans were his allies in Italy. William the Conqueror, who invaded England with papal approval, acted in his newly acquired domain as the head of the Church and without opposition from the Archbishop Lanfranc. Friction came only in the next reign between Henry I and Anselm. The ultimate compromise resembled the Concordat of Worms.

— 5 —

DEUS VULT

The great monastic reform of Cluny, as we have seen, envisaged the reform of the monasteries, the reform of the Church and the reform of the world. The latter meant the suppression of the interminable feudal warfare fostered by political decentralization and constant barbarian raids. The theory of the just war formulated by St. Augustine quite broke down under these circumstances. He had declared that war must be just on one side only, and the justice should be determined by the prince. But who was the prince in a society where everyone except the emperor was under someone else and everyone except the serf over someone else? Strictly speaking, the use of force by a superior against an inferior was either what we should call police force or else tyranny. An attack by an inferior on a superior was rebellion. The term war could be applied only to conflicts between equals, but even so, if one party were attacked, could he directly defend himself without first appealing for redress to the overlord of his foe, and must he also get permission from his own superior? The practical answer was to jettison the code and, if struck, to strike back.

Augustine's ethic also excluded the clergy from the exercise of arms—above all, the monks, and obviously the nuns. But in the Middle Ages bishops put armor over their cassocks, monks put helmets over their cowls, and nuns behaved like Amazons. And prince-bishops, of course, were geared into the whole feudal structure. The reformers saw no way to deal with this situation save by voluntary renunciation. To try to suppress war altogether appeared unrealistic, but limitations might be imposed. The Truce of God forbade fighting on weekends, on holy days and during the whole of Lent; the open season for feuding was reduced to the summer months. The Peace of God applied to persons, seeking to increase the number of the non-combatants. There should be no attack upon clerics, pilgrims, merchants, women, the aged, farmers, oxen, asses and agricultural implements. In a word, the clerical, commercial, agricultural and female elements of the populace were to be exempt. Princes took an oath to observe these rules. (*See Reading No. 4, II B.*)

The promises may have done some good, perhaps less to create virtue than to instill a sense of guilt. Richard Coeur de Lion, for example, met his death from an arrow of his own returned by an archer of a rebellious vassal whom Richard was endeavoring to subdue during Lent. Contemporaries—and probably Richard, too—thought that the random shot was a divine judgment for fighting out of season. But however much he may have recognized the hand of God after being hit, he was not deterred in advance. There were many like him who vowed and failed. Then the Church stimulated the formation of a peace militia in which the clergy served both in France and in Germany to discipline the violators. This was a radical new departure. One might say that the Church was not taking part in war because this was police action, but that is a modern distinction. The Church had grasped the sword and was encroaching on the normal role of the state. In one instance in Germany the peace army got out of hand and ravaged the country. A count had to raise a counter-army to discipline the peace army, and in the ensuing conflict seven hundred of the clergy were left upon the field. Implicit in all of these attempts to enforce the peace was the idea of a holy war instituted by the Church. All ambiguity was dispelled at the Council of Clermont in 1095 A.D. when Urban II began his speech in the vein of the great pleas for peace of the last fifty years. Let the Christian nobles of France stop devouring each other. Let them instead unite and go against the common enemy of the faith, the infidels defiling the holy places and impeding the pilgrims. (*See Reading No. 4, III A.*) And all the assembly cried "*Dieux le veult, Deus vult,* God wills it."

The Crusades. The inauguration of the crusades marked a thoroughly new attitude on the part of the Church to warfare. The use of arms by priests, monks and nuns had been regarded earlier in the Middle Ages as an abuse. The effort to enforce the Peace and the Truce of God could be construed as the maintainance of the peace, but a foreign war against the enemies of the faith constituted a new category even as to war. The just war aimed to vindicate justice in terms of life and property. The crusade was fought for an ideal, for the faith, or at least for freedom to exercise the faith. The war was initiated not by the state, but by the Church. The citizen served not so much at the command of the prince, but voluntarily by taking the cross. The traditional code of humanity in war broke down in fighting with an enemy of the faith. The crusade marked the ultimate militarization of Christianity, and the most glaring mark of the change was that even a priest might fight without qualms or penance.

The later crusades did come to be under royal auspices, but the first was the work of the pope, though to be sure princes took the cross in response to his plea. The success of the crusade was largely the work of the papal party, and it was a genuine achievement in European unity—or rather in French unity, seeing that the first crusade was exclusively French. There were four parties politically independent: the northern Normans and the southern Normans, the northern French of the *Langue de oil* and the southern French of Languedoc. They journeyed by separate routes and converged on Constantinople. There they had to swear allegiance to the eastern emperor, to the disgruntlement especially of the papal party. After an initial victory on the Asian side of the Dardanelles, the crusaders had little difficulty in reaching Syria, because of the sympathy of the native Christian populace. But as they advanced, their own divisions became apparent. It was clear that the chieftains were more interested in carving out principalities for themselves in the Holy Land, as their Viking forebears had done in Normandy and Sicily, than in reaching the Holy Sepulchre. The papal party was largely responsible for holding them together until Jerusalem fell in 1099 A.D., and the crusaders broke into a paean of jubilation that God had thus vindicated His holy religion. (*See Reading No. 4, III B.*)

Cistercian Movement. Coincident with this outburst of militant zeal came new upsurges of monastic reform, at first glance at variance with the Gregorian papacy and the crusades, yet actually in many ways quite comparable. There were three such movements: the Carthusian, the Premonstratian and the Cistercian. The latter alone can engage us. Citeaux was founded in the year before the fall of Jerusalem, *i.e.* in 1098 A.D. As the name indicates, it was French. The ideal of Citeaux was to withdraw from the world much more than Cluny had ever done. No longer should stables and fodder be in constant readiness for a couple of dozen steeds. Citeaux was not to be overrun by cavalcades of greedy-bellied nobles and their retainers. Neither was Cluny to be caught up in the prayer mill which spent the day so everlastingly in oraisons that no time was left for the contemplation of Him to whom the prayers were directed. The Cluniacs must have wearied of the continual round, and one can sympathize with those who diverted themselves by dropping melted candle wax from the top choir onto the shaven crowns below. The Cistercians were resolved, like the old Benedictines, to take time for the delights of contemplation and ecstatic reveries.

The most renowned of all the early Cistercians was St. Bernard, and he is one of the greatest of the medieval mystics. In him the romantic movement captured piety. His sermons on the Canticles are redolent of the imagery of the bridegroom and the bride, and if he did not write the hymn "Jesus, the very thought of thee with sweetness fills my breast," nevertheless his mellifluous prose, rhythmic and sonorous, inspired a school of hymnody. (*See Reading 5, II A.*) Citeaux desired meditation and Citeaux abhorred distraction. No more of the grotesque statuary which adorned—Bernard said defaced—the Romanesque churches and abbeys! If the common folk must have some external excitation, let them be pardoned, but those who had advanced upon the mystic way should rather gaze than gape. Stained-glass windows were likewise deemed a distraction, and lofty churches, with vast empty spaces, were rather a monument to the pride of man than an aid in the ascent to God. (*See Reading No. 5, III.*) Above all, Citeaux eschewed wealth, luxury and laxity. Back to poverty, back to simplicity, back to rigor!

The Cistercians were resolved to restore manual labor. They would not accept huge productive estates already manned with serfs. If, indeed, they accepted land with laborers, they expelled the laborers and replaced them by the innovation of lay brothers, unlearned men, peasants, instead of the aristocracy who had largely manned the earlier orders. But this did not mean that the monks themselves were exempt from the labor of their hands. St. Bernard wrought like any serf. By preference, the Cistercians took unbroken land. They felled forests and drained swamps, reclaiming enough land vitally to affect the economy of the north. They experimented with crops and constructed greenhouses for testing plants. When land was irreclaimable they turned to grazing, clothing themselves in the white, undyed wool of their sheep. But one cannot wear an unlimited amount of wool. The husbandry of the monks produced beyond their needs, and they began to dispose of the surplus. They even contracted in advance to supply so much, and in case of inability they borrowed at interest. Such transactions brought them into competition with the laity, and in the course of a couple of centuries they were scarcely distinguished from other orders. But once more let it be said that an order is not to be judged by its decline. The virtues of the Cistercians were their undoing, but long before they were undone they had contributed substantially to Europe's economy.

But of course neither they nor anyone else conceived of this as their primary task. The community esteemed their prayers as highly as once they had done those of the Cluniacs, for the Cistercians enjoyed the special favor of the Virgin Mary. A visitor to heaven was amazed at first to find no Cistercians until he discovered that they were concealed beneath the folds of Mary's robe. And though they sought a greater retirement from the world, they came to be highly influential in its affairs.

St. Bernard here also is the great example. He was quite as much a European figure as Odilo. Bernard dominated councils, invaded universities, chided princes, corresponded with crowned heads and chided a pope who had come from his own abbey. Indeed, there was no pope of that period who wielded an influence comparable to that of Bernard. An excellent example is afforded by his role in the resolution of a papal schism. Anacletus II may have been more regularly elected, but Innocent II won Bernard's endorsement as the better man. But next of all came the persuasion of the crowned heads of Europe not only to accept the right pope, but to renounce all the local bishops adhering to the wrong one. Bernard, having persuaded the German emperor and the French and English kings, then turned to William of Aquitaine, who was obstinate in his adherence to the wrong local bishop. Bernard excommunicated William, then went to the church and celebrated the miracle of the mass. William stood by the outer door. Bernard, having consecrated the sacred elements, took them in his hands and striding to the door confronted William with the words, "Before you is your Judge before whom you will stand in the last day. Do you dare to despise Him as you have despised His servants?" William fell foaming at the mouth. There remained only Roger the Norman of Sicily. His lawyers began to adduce canonical arguments. Bernard cut them off. "Was there," he demanded, "more than one ark in which Noah was saved? That ark was the Church. But now we have two arks. In one we have the king of France, the emperor of Germany, the king of England and the duke of Aquitaine together with that worthy pope Innocent. In the other we have that unholy pope Anacletus and Roger the Norman. Now which do you think is the true ark?" Roger changed arks.

The Cistercian movement provides, after all, a parallel to the Gregorian papacy. Both sought separation from the world—the papacy by rejecting lay appointments. And both sought to dominate the world. When Christianity takes itself seriously, it must either forsake or master the world and at different points may try to do both at once. The papacy did, and the Cistercians did. The similarity is most obvious in their attitude to the crusade, for the second crusade was in large measure the work of St. Bernard. He it was who with perfervid pleas incited the men of arms in France to cleanse the holy precincts of pagan filth, assuring them that to conquer was glorious, to die was gain. Bernard is credited with having composed the rule for the Templars. This was the ultimate fusion of Teutonic valor and the Christian warfare. Now even militarism and monasticism had been blended. The monk in armor received consecration at the hands of the Church.

The second crusade, incidentally, was a fiasco and contributed to a revulsion of feeling in which many began to say *Deus non vult.* (*See Reading No. 4, III C.*)

Gothic Architecture. This same century saw the beginning of Gothic architecture. The first example is commonly taken to be the abbey church at St. Denis, rebuilt in this new style by Bernard's great contemporary, the Abbot Suger. He was a very different type from Bernard, a man who did not hesitate to be both an abbot and the regent of France, though perhaps the two men were not so different at this point. Bernard could rule France without being a regent. But Suger's abbey appeared lax to Bernard, who addressed to him an unsweetened remonstrance. (*See Reading No. 5, III.*) Suger took it graciously and introduced reforms, but he was still a different spirit and reveled in that magnificence of churchly architecture which Bernard regarded as at best a concession and at worst a snare.

But what was the genius of the Gothic? As to this there is much debate. Some say it was an imitation of the soaring evergreens of the northern forests, and had there not been a Christian Gothic there might just as well have been a pagan Gothic. Others retort, "Nonsense! Gothic did not originate in the northern forests, but on the Île de France." Still, the trees supplied the pattern—not evergreens, but deciduous trees, whose leafy tracery was transferred to the graceful configurations of the windows.

But others again say that not nature but philosophy determined the new mode, Neoplatonic philosophy with its doctrine of the metaphysics of light, according to which light is a form impressed upon objects, conferring upon them visibility, a form which in fact determines the relation of spaces. Light again is the most immaterial aspect of the material, infusing into the material the quality of the divine. The experience of light is contact with God. Therefore the wall of the church must become diaphanous. The source of these ideas was none other than the patron saint of France and of the abbey, St. Denis, Dionysius the Areopagite, whose writing is replete with the imagery of light, which again recurs in the poems of Suger. All of this may perchance be so, though scarcely quite in the manner alleged. The specific doctrine of the metaphysics of light does not appear either in Dionysius or in Suger. What one does find in them is the age-old metaphor of light for spiritual insight. In the Psalms we read, "Send forth Thy light," (Ps. 42) and in the gospels, "I am the light of the world" (Jn. 9:5). Observe, moreover, that Suger said that he had introduced windows that they might serve to enhance the splendor that was within, namely of the jewels. (*See Reading No. 5, V.*)

Wherein then lies the genius of Gothic? Others answer that it is the expression of the western spirit, which renounces repose and will not rest in the harmony of a Greek temple, but achieves indeed a structural stability suggesting, however, but a momentary equilibrium in which faith and reason, logic and aspiration, precise lines and luminous haze, thrust and counterthrust, sustain each other by a balance of opposites, just as in scholasticism the affirmation and the denial are resolved in a response, only to give rise to another series. Here is the spirit of man precariously soaring in his ventures with the untried.

But is this Christian? Some say no. This striving is only the *hybris* of man seeking to scale the battlements of heaven. Yet this is not an adequate explanation, because at this point Gothic had to reckon with failure. The observation has been made that the question to put to the guide in a medieval cathedral is this, "When did the tower fall down?" St. Michel fell twice. The masons had to come to terms with the stone's weight and the earth's pull. They could not go on with indefinite soaring. Failing then to achieve actual height, they developed devices for creating the illusion of height. The ribbed vault, the groined arch suggested the unresolved. The column was not a massive pillar of stone, but a cluster of shafts whose many lines carried the eye aloft. Flying buttresses without made possible the reduction of the sustaining wall to a narrow aspiring lith. Gothic is the leap after the illimitable, the grasping of the finite for the infinite.

The statuary of the Gothic illustrates another aspect of the Neoplatonic influence with its disparagement of the physical. There are distinctions in the physical. There is the sensuous and there is the sexless, passionless, reflective, contemplative, brooding on the myteries of existence, lost in the abyss of the ineffable. Take the John the Baptist at Chartres. This has been called the greatest John the Baptist ever carved. That depends. The John the Baptist of Rodin is also great. But it is another John the Baptist. There were two types in the New Testament. There is the John who came striding out of the desert to hurl woes at a brood of vipers. This is the John of Rodin. And there is that other John who saw the heavens opened and the dove descending and who exclaimed, "Behold the lamb of God that taketh away the sins of the world." This is the John of Chartres.

And this explains why the Cistercians could adopt Gothic after all, though with simplifications. They would have no stained glass, only opaque white glass, yet leaded together with exquisite tracery. But surely the Cistercians missed something in their austerity. The stained glass— azure, ruby, opalescent, storied with the lore of the patri- archs, apostles, evangelists, martyrs and saints, authentic and legendary, the depiction of the passion, the ascension, the glorification of the Son of God, the coronation of the Virgin, the supreme glory of the Lord of all the universe, God the Father almighty, the maker of heaven and earth, surrounded by all the company of the heavenly host, where seraphim and cherubim continually do cry, "Holy, holy, holy, Lord God of Sabbaoth"—who could behold all this without feeling himself to be lifted into the com- pany of the redeemed who stand encircled about the throne of God?

— 6 —

THE PEAK OF THE PAPACY

The conflicts of Church and state did not cease with the investiture controversy. In the eleventh century a ve- hement quarrel broke out between King Henry II of Eng- land and his one-time crony Thomas à Becket, whom he made the archibishop of Canterbury, thinking thereby to control the Church. But Becket was imbued with the

medieval concept of vassalage. When he was the king's
man, he served the king. When he became the *villain* of
God, then God he served. The dispute was over the im-
munity of the clergy from the jurisdiction of the secular
courts. Henry was willing that the guilt of clerics should
be determined in ecclesiastical courts, but if the accused
were adjudged guilty he should be turned over to civil
justice. Now civil justice was brutal. Twenty men might
be seen hanging from the same gallows for minor offenses,
whereas the Church never inflicted the penalty of death.
One way to mitigate the barbarity of the civil law was to
extend the scope of the canon law. Many claimed benefit
of clergy with minimal qualification. The tonsure was not
sufficient proof of clerical status, since anyone could clip
his hair. The common test was ability to read the first
verse of the fifty-first Psalm: "Have mercy upon me, O
God, according to Thy loving kindness." One scamp had
the passage memorized. The judge trapped him by hand-
ing him the book upside down. To insist on clerical im-
munity and to wink at dubious clericalism was one way
of mitigating the law. But one could wish that Becket had
been a clear-cut martyr for humanity instead of for im-
munity. His martyrdom slowed the drive for impartial
justice and did little or nothing to humanize the law.

Another conflict was between the Emperor Frederick
Barbarossa and several popes, notably Alexander III. It
was partly a quarrel over a mistranslation from Latin into
German, so that the emperor was declared to receive his
empire as a fief from the papacy. This semantic snarl was
disentangled, but there remained a bitter contest over the
estates bequeathed by the Countess Matilda to the Church
and now claimed by the empire, a quarrel complicated by
the rise to independence of the north Italian cities, each
of which came to have an imperial faction called Ghibelline and a papal faction called Guelf. Frederick several
times made an incursion into Italy to subdue them, but at
Legnano in 1176 A.D. he was roundly defeated by the
Lombard League, and not long after was drowned on the
third crusade. The papacy reaped the victory.

Innocent III.   Onto this foundation stepped the
pope who for prestige and power was the greatest of all
time, Innocent III. His authority was not automatic. He
held the lid on a boiling cauldron by pressures now from

thumbs, now from fingers, and seldom without blisters. First he succeeded in making his candidate the emperor. It is a tangled story of a contest between Guelf and Ghibelline. The maneuvers of Innocent brought the dignity to Frederick II, who as an infant on the death of his father had been reared by his mother in Sicily as a ward of the pope.

In every country of Europe, Innocent scored one victory after another. In France, Philip Augustus was compelled to renounce his concubine and take back his lawful wife, the Danish princess Ingeborg. This was another loveless marriage of state. When Philip first saw his affianced, he said, a shiver went down his spine. But to have been married was to have been married, and when Philip put her aside the pope laid his territory under an interdict. This was a geographical excommunication applied to the area in which the culprit resided. In his territory the rites of the Church were either forbidden or restricted. In this instance only baptism and the viaticum were allowed. Masses ceased. The dead could not be buried. There was some doubt whether marriages would be valid and those who could went outside the jurisdiction. Nothing could render a king so odious as that his presence should deprive his subjects of salvation. Philip capitulated.

On the other hand, a royal marriage between Aragon and Castile was dissolved because of consanguinity. The Church forbade unions sometimes to the seventh, more commonly to the sixth degree of cousinship, and also between those spiritually related through baptism. (*See Reading No. 2, VIII.*) Such unions required a dispensation from the pope, and if later a flaw were discovered in the grant, or worse if a relationship previously unsuspected came to light, the union was severed, no matter how attached the parties might be to each other.

In the Spanish peninsula the pope so united the three Christian kings that Castile in the center, flanked by Aragon and Navarre, could repulse the Saracens at the battle of Navas de Tolosa. Portugal became a fief of the papacy. So also did England, but only after a violent controversy. King John insisted on appointing the Archbishop of Canterbury. The pope insisted that the monks should elect Stephen Langton and, if John would not concur, threatened an interdict. John swore by the teeth of God that he would slit the noses of all the clerics in England if they refused to perform the holy rites. John might have continued in his defiance had not Philip Augustus, his overlord, been ready to undertake a crusade against him. Observe the transfer of the crusading idea back to Europe. John stooped to conquer, made England a fief of the papacy, and thereby forestalled a French invasion. When later the barons presented him with Magna Carta, though they were headed by Stephen Langton, the king appealed to his overlord the pope, who declined to recognize the charter because it had not been negotiated through him.

Innocent had dealings with all of the fringe countries of Europe, intervening to insure legitimate successions to thrones, defending bishops against kings, insisting on the right of asylum, temporarily reconciling to Rome the churches of Bulgaria, Armenia and Syria. He chose a husband for the queen of Jerusalem, accorded rights and imposed restrictions upon the Jews, summoned the great Lateran Council, the Fourth, which promulgated the doctrine of transsubstantiation. (*See Reading No. 6, IE.*) Surely it was no accident that sacramentalism should have reached the peak coincidentally with sacerdotalism. The power of the priest rests upon his ability to mediate to men the saving grace of the sacraments. The whole theocratic and hierarchic structure of society, alike in Church and state, outlined by Dionysius the Areopagite (*see Reading No. 3, VI*), is sacramental. By these sacred rites the celestial hierarchy transmits its divine power to the terrestrial. (Compare p. 28.)

Note, incidentally, the diverse meanings given to the word theocratic. Literally, it means the rule of God. Sometimes it is applied to a Christian society in which the state takes the lead and the emperor is regarded as directly God's appointee. Thus, the empire of Charlemagne is called theocratic. But sometimes again it is applied to a Christian society in which the pope exercises the greatest authority. Hence, the term "the papal theocracy," nowhere better exemplified than under Innocent III. The authority which he exercised was not based, however, on the claim to direct temporal jurisdiction over all the world. To be sure, in those kingdoms which were fiefs of the papacy—Sicily, Portugal and England—he was the immediate overlord, but elsewhere he declared that he

THE PEAK OF THE PAPACY

judged not the fief but the sin. (*See Reading No. 6, 1.*) But
since sin is quite prevalent, this gave him a wide area of
jurisdiction. That he was able to exercise it without arms
of his own, by the sheer weight of spiritual authority over
a domain as vast and even greater than that of Charlemagne, is witness to the power of an ideal.

But he was not always successful in terms of what he
wanted to do. The fourth crusade was a glittering fiasco.
The crusaders bargained with Venice for their transporta-
tion. Since they could not pay, she accepted in lieu the
subjugation of her rebellious vassal city, Zara on the Dal-
matian coast. But Zara was Christian. The pope excommunicated the crusaders. They proceeded blithely to Constantinople, became involved in a quarrel between rival
aspirants to the imperial dignity, besieged and took the
city, scoured the altars of orthodox defilement and celebrated the Latin rite. The pope made the best out of a
deplorable miscarriage and appointed a Latin patriarch.
This forcible subjugation of Constantinople lasted some
seventy years and served only to embitter the relations
between the eastern and western churches.

Resurgence of Heresy. Much more grievous was
the outbreak of heresy in southern France. It began earlier
than the time of Innocent, but in his day had become
formidable. Why splits should have occurred when the
papacy had reached its peak is a puzzle. The Middle Ages
after the invasions had known no schisms and only a
handful of individual heretics. This was all very different
from the situation in the early Church, which had some
eighty divisions. Why the sectarian motif should have
subsided for roughly eight hundred years invites conjec-
ture. Perhaps the decline in culture diminished the interest
in theology, but still churchmen can quarrel over more
subjects than theology. Perhaps the struggle with paganism consumed all energies. Perhaps monasticism provided
an adequate outlet for variety. At any rate, we encounter
only sporadic notices of heretics after the year 1000 A.D.
in France, with an increasing number in the twelfth century. From then on, southern France and northern Italy—
and, by and by, England and Bohemia—pullulated with
sects up and into the time of the Reformation. Very plau-
sibly, these movements are to be regarded as the obverse
of the great reformatory endeavors of Cluny, Citeaux and

the Gregorian, with their effort to reform the orders, the
Church and the world. Gregory's demand that the laity
refuse to take the sacraments from concubinous priests
could easily be interpreted to mean that the sacrament
would be inefficacious if administered by the unworthy.

These reforms had all in a measure failed of their ob-
jectives. The Gregorian had imposed clerical celibacy, and
the result was widespread clerical concubinage. The Cluny
movement had sponsored the Truce and the Peace of
God, and the issue was a holy war, followed by disillusion-
ment as to whether God had willed it after all. The Gregorian reform aspired to give churchly direction to civil
affairs, and the outcome was the proclamation of a crusade to drive the French out of Sicily. If then the monastic
orders and the papacy could not adequately carry through
their own program, the time had come for "a reformation
without tarrying for any," to borrow a slogan from the
Puritan revolution. Often those who so spoke were lay-
men, making extensive use of the vernaculars. Sometimes,
as in England and Bohemia, sectarianism became conjoined with nationalist sentiment.

Certain ideas contributed to the dissolution of the universal Church. One was the revival of primitive Christian
eschatology with its expectation of the imminent end of
the age. In the twelfth century, Joachim of Fiore divided
history into three ages of the Father, the Son and the Holy
Ghost, and each age into seven periods. He believed that
he was in the sixth period of the second age and therefore
the third was about to break. As a date he assigned the
year 1260 A.D., corresponding to the number of days
spent in the wilderness by the woman in the Apocalypse.
If then the great institutional church were about to be
superseded by the church of the Spirit, plainly her utility
and prestige were diminished. Another idea was the doctrine of predestination. It is innocuous if there is no way
of telling who is predestined, but if there is a way of
knowing who at any rate are the rejected and if by a
moral test one may say that reprehensible popes are the
reprobates, then they may be identified with the mythical
figure of Antichrist. These ideas were to appear in Wyclif
and Hus. Eschatology undercuts the Church from ahead
and predestination from behind. The sects in general attacked sacerdotalism and almost inevitably, therefore, the

sacramentalism on which it rested. Particularly, they attacked the mass.

Waldenses and Cathari. One of the first of these sects was the Waldensian, named for Waldo, a merchant of Lyons in the late twelfth century. He gave his goods to feed the poor, and to this, of course, the Church had no objection. Then, however, he engaged a priest to translate for him portions of the Scripture into the vernacular. These he memorized and began to teach and preach. For this, permission was needed. Some of his followers applied to Pope Alexander III at the Lateran Council in 1176 A.D. Walter Mapes gives an account of the examination. (*See Reading No. 6, III.*) These simple folk, who "naked followed the naked Christ," were rejected because of their simplicity, but they refused to be suppressed. Among their tenets was a close adherence to the Sermon on the Mount, with no oath and no revenge. They all begged until, rejected by the Church and denied alms, they had to develop a supporting branch of their own. Rooted out of southern France, they found a refuge in the highest habitable regions of the Alps, where they survived until the edict of toleration in 1870 enabled them to spread over Italy. Torre Pelice is their present center. Some have come to North and some to South America, notably Paraguay.

Very different were the Cathari, because their ideas were definitely heretical, having been imported from Bulgaria. A few of their number were burned by mobs in France as early as the eleventh century, but the large influx is to be attributed to crusaders returning disillusioned from the east. The Cathari, called also Albigenses from the town of Albi, stand in the succession which runs thus: Gnostics, Manichees, Paulicians, Bogomili, Cathari. These groups all have in common a sharp dualism between spirit and matter, and often also between God and the devil. Since matter is evil and the world is material, the world is evil, and was not created by a good but rather by a malevolent deity. The Old Testament, which describes approvingly the creation, is the work of this demiurge. The New Testament is totally different, the book of the Most High God, uncontaminated by the physical. Everything connected with sex is evil, and nothing related to the processes of sex should be eaten, such as eggs, milk and cheese. Happily the Cathari did not know that fish and plants have sex. No new children should .be brought into the world because birth entails imprisonment in the flesh. To have sexual relations without children is evil, but not so evil as to incarcerate fresh souls. After death, souls transmigrate into other bodies. No life should be taken because this may mean a less favorable reincarnation. A device used to detect a Cathar was to find whether he would kill a chicken.

The Cathari considered themselves Christians; they accepted the New Testament, but rejected the authority, the hierarchy, liturgy and sacraments of the Catholic Church. They also rejected images, including the cross—who would revere the gallows on which his father was hanged? And they rejected music, indeed all sensory aids to religion, whether through the mouth, in the case of the mass, the eye or the ear. The Cathari were noted for the gravity of their ascetic deportment. (*See Reading No. 6, II.*)

Innocent III tried to incite Raymond of Toulouse, the lord of Provence and the clergy of the Midi against the heretics, but with little success. His excoriation of the archbishop of Narbonne for abetting heresy by his evil example was scorching. (*See Reading No. 6, II A.*) The Catholics esteemed their Catharan neighbors, and many of the noble houses were riddled with heresy. A papal legate campaigning in the region was assassinated and accomplished more when dead than alive. A crusade was then launched with a promise of an indulgence in return for forty days of service. Hordes from northern France poured into the Midi ravaging, pillaging, burning heretics *magno cum gaudio* (with huge delight). When a town was being besieged, the abbot of Citeaux was asked how, when it fell, the Cathari were to be distinguished from the Catholics. "Kill them all," he answered. "God will know His own." The outcome was the crushing of heresy, the devastation of Provence and the eventual annexation of the territory to the crown of France.

The Inquisition. To deal with the remnants of the Waldenses and the Cathari, the Inquisition was established by Gregory IX in the 1220's. There had been earlier episcopal inquisitions, but the bishops were too tender of their neighbors. The new Inquisition was papal. The theory was that heresy constitutes the most heinous of all crimes. The enormity of an offense depends in part on the rank of the person against whom it is committed. God is the supreme person. An offense against Him is the supreme offense. Heresy is worse than any crime on earth, worse than matricide because against our Mother the Church, worse than treason because against the King of heaven, worse than counterfeiting because it simulates falsely the truth of God. Heresy damns souls and brings upon the community which allows it the displeasure of the Almighty. All of the penalties imposed for lesser crimes may with greater reason be inflicted for the greater. If the counterfeiter loses his hands and the traitor goes to the gallows, why not the heretic to the stake? For him the penalty was burning because the Church abhors the shedding of blood. The Church, however, did not inflict any physical penalty, but turned the condemned over to the secular arm with a plea for mercy (and, if it were granted, punished the official by excommunication). Such severity was deemed entirely consonant with love, for if the heretic recanted out of fear, his soul was saved. If he were obdurate, half an hour at the stake was only a foretaste of eternity, and by his ordeal multitudes might be deterred and saved. Many devices were used to extort confessions, long periods of solitary confinement, protracted uncertainty, threats to relatives and torture. All of this was deemed an aspect of the cure of souls and was done in the name of love. Grievous is the reflection that the methods used today by totalitarian powers to break down resisters are only a technological refinement of the methods used by the medieval Church in order to safeguard the truth of Christ and vindicate the honor of God. (*See Reading No. 6, III.*)

Dominicans and Franciscans. But happily these were not the only methods employed. In this same period arose two new monastic orders, one of them in particular with the intent of combating heresy by persuasion and the power of truth. This was the Dominican. Somewhat different in emphasis was the Franciscan. Dominic was a Spaniard traveling with his bishop in the Midi. Speedily he was convinced that the ascetic heretics would not be reclaimed by bishops with an imposing equipage. Poverty commended itself as a strategic device. Yet the great tool was not mere poverty, but sound doctrine. The Dominicans were to be teachers. The letters after the name of a Dominican namely O.P., Order of Preachers, might better have been given to a Franciscan, with the letters O.D., Order of Doctors, for the Dominican Thomas Aquinas was of their number.

The story is told that Dominic was once interrupted in his studies by the chirping of a sparrow. He caught and plucked the bird. One may be confident that the tale is not true, but it would never have been told of St. Francis. He would not have been studying, and he would not have harmed any winged creature. St. Francis exhibits a blend of reaction against and accommodation to his age. He was in revolt against its commercialism. His father was a merchant of Assisi, a representative of the new mercantile class arising along with the revival of cities, commerce and coinage after the crusades. Francis, even before his conversion, loathed his father's niggardly getting and spending. A gay blade was Francis, who, after masquerading as the king of fools, was found one night seated in dejection on a curb. "What's the matter?" mocked his companions. "Have you gotten married?" "Yes," said Francis, "to the fairest of all brides, *la Donna Poverta,* the Lady of Poverty." She was an abstraction, a personification to whom he addressed the romantic love current among the troubadors of Provence, where his mother was born. But her regime was no abstraction, for it required of him an absolute renunciation of all possessions, coupled with a readiness either to beg or to work, but never for alms or wages in excess of the needs of a day. Francis would not be undone, like the older monastic orders, either by donations or by diligence. A little company gathered about him, and to his rule they were committed. Their program was to tend the lepers, assist the peasants and, above all else, to preach—to people where they were in the centers of population. Instead of the Benedictine *stabilitas,* the Franciscans and the Dominicans called for *mobilitas.* They would invade parishes and do the work which the priests neglected. In this respect they were accommodating themselves to the circumstances of their age. Their program also required permission. Both secured it from Innocent III, who may well have recalled the mistake of Alexander III, who, had he treated the Waldenses more tenderly, might have made of them a new order of the Catholic Church. Innocent blessed the *Poverello.*

The piety of Francis was Gothic in its thrusts and counterthrusts. His religion was lyrical with joy. Poverty spelled emancipation from care and contention. By renouncing all, he possessed all, the whole creation. There was in him none of the Catharan despising of the world. Francis composed the first vernacular poem in the Italian language in praise of the Creator, the creation and all the creatures, our brother the sun and our sister the moon, our sisters the stars, mother earth, brother fire and herbs and plants of divers colors. In this reveling in nature, some in our day have seen a line running to the Renaissance. Yet also in Francis one finds the cult of pain. He so meditated on the passion of Christ that on his body appeared the semblance of his wounds, the stigmata. The passion had at last become the core of the piety of the west. Did it arise perhaps from a sense of guilt for all the sensuality and violence of the preceding centuries, for which only the blood of the Redeemer could atone? Man now saw his ugliness and cried to be redeemed through pain, the Redeemer's and his own. In meek endurance is the perfect joy. (*See Reading No. 6, IV.*) In the age of Francis the crucifix was changed, no longer the draped and passionless incarnation of cosmic repose as in the Byzantine, but the man naked save for a loin cloth, legs crossed and held by only one nail that the twisted pose might the more convey the writhing agony. Francis, the troubador of God, who preached to the birds and tamed the wolf of Gubbio, bore in his body the marks of the Lamb that was slain.

How he would have grieved had he lived to see the strife that would ensue in his order! When he died, brother Elias sought to honor him by erecting a beautiful basilica at Assisi. Churh building is costly and a money box was installed. Brother Leo smashed it. Then began the conflict between the Conventuals and the Spirituals. The Conventuals were the sensible ones. They saw very well that begging only for the day and every day was all very well so long as the brothers were no more than a dozen, but it was not feasible for five hundred. If one could not keep anything over from a fat day, some days would be painfully lean. They were ready to accept the compromise proposed by Cardinal Ugolini that the Church should have the *dominium,* the lordship over property, and confer on the friars the *usus,* that is the use. But the Spirituals insisted on the *regola senza glossa,* the rule without a gloss.

To make an absolute out of the rule of St. Francis con-
flicted with the authority of the Church. Some of the Spirituals became rebels, called Fraticelli, and some of the
sons of Francis were burned by the Inquisition.

— 7 —

THE FAITH

Much has already been said about the faith of the
Church, especially the faith in the sacraments and the
power of excommunication and interdict, the faith that
through the sacraments the grace of the celestial hierarchy is transmitted to the terrestrial. But a vast number
of other questions arose concerning the faith, as to the
ground of knowledge, the relation of faith and reason, the
existence and characteristics of God, the nature of man,
the reason for the incarnation and redemption, the con-
summation of all things, the relations of Church and state.

The twelfth century is the period when the theological
interest was notably revived. To be sure, there had been
theologians earlier in the Middle Ages: Boethius, Gregory
I, Alcuin, Scotus Erigena, not to forget the few heretics
for whom we have not had time. But the great renaissance
belongs to the age of the founding of Citeaux, the second
crusade and the beginning of Gothic. Both a result and a
cause of the new movement was the founding of universities, growing out of the cathedral schools. Two of the first
great figures were Anselm and Abelard. Both were, in the
first instance, believers who desired to be able to give a
reason for the faith that was in them. *"Credo ut intelli-
gam,"* said Anselm, "I believe that I may understand."
Anselm was a man of devotion, deeply troubled when his
cogitations disturbed his meditations. (*See Readings No.
5, I A-C.*) Abelard is always reputed to have been the
great rationalist of his day because of his book *Sic et Non,*

Yes and No (*see Reading No. 5, I D*), in which he set
forth contradictions in the writings of the Church fathers.
The purpose was not to discredit the faith, but to resolve
the discrepancies. They were of two sorts. Some were indeed contradictions among the doctors, but some were
paradoxes in the very being of God. The procedure was
to set up a conflict and then strive by dialectic to resolve
it. This was the age of logic, of confidence in man's ability, albeit limited, to extract truth from truth. Anselm and
Abelard are the fabricators of the scholastic method.

But scholasticism was more than a method. It had substance. The term may, of course, be defined as whatever
was taught in the *schola,* the school, but more commonly
it is taken to refer to the content of orthodox theology.
As such it lies between two extremes, the monism de-
rivative from the Arab Averroists and the dualism of the
Cathari. Scholasticism is pluralistic, positing the existence
of God and of the creatures whose identity is never
merged in the abyss of the deity. But within scholasticism,
as thus defined, there were three main lines. Central may
be called the Thomistic, which runs from Abelard through
Peter Lombard and Albertus Magnus to St. Thomas. On
the right may be placed the so-called Augustinians—
whether they really reproduced the theology of Augustine
need not detain us. The representatives are Anselm, the
Victorines and Bonaventura. To the left we may assign
the school of the Nominalists, represented in the twelfth
century by Roscellin and in the fourteenth and fifteenth
by William of Ockham and his followers.

They differed first of all as to the nature of reality. The
Augustinians, tinged with Platonism, were the realists who
believed in the reality of universals, like the Platonic ideas,
existing in the mind of God anterior to any concretion in
particulars, *universalia ante rem.* From this point of view
the Church, the state and the family are entities anteced-
ent to their historical manifestations. The middle position,
called moderate realism, believed that reality is not dis-
jointed. There are universals, but they do not exist apart
from their concretion in particulars. They are *universalia
in re.* The third view held that reality consists of unrelated
particulars, related actually only by contiguity in place
and time. Categories are mere names, *nomina,* hence the
term Nominalism. From this point of view Church, state

and family become fortuitous, temporary, voluntary associations. The state and marriage are formed by contract and the Church by covenant. The implicit sociological consequences of these positions may account for the zeal and acrimony with which they were debated in a society struggling to emerge from the atomistic tendencies of a disrupted order into a recovery of the vanished unities. Realism in philosophy was on the side of universalism, centralization and even absolutism. Nominalism favored decentralization, individualism and perhaps even schism. Moderate realism comported best with a balance in society between centralization and decentralization, the universal and the individual. Here is an example in philosophy and in society of the principle of thrust and counterthrust.

Associated with these positions were variant views as to the way in which man can know God. The Augustinians, with their Platonic and Neoplatonic strains, believed in the full demonstrability of God's existence. The famous argument of Anselm is called the ontological. The reasoning is that a being greater than which cannot be conceived must exist because that which exists is greater than that which does not exist. If, then, that than which a greater cannot be conceived does not exist, one can conceive of that which does also exist and is therefore necessarily greater. (*See Reading No. 5, I A.*) One suspects that the cogency of this argument is not unrelated to the belief of the Augustinians in the possibility of the vision of God in this life. If there can be such immediacy of rapport, if man to this degree participates in the divine being, then the leap is reduced from what is conceived to that which is. In that case, faith and knowledge are not mutually exclusive. One may at the same time know God and believe in God. Faith and knowledge are simply different modes of apprehension.

The moderate realists, in the line leading to St. Thomas, rejected the possibility of the vision of God and rejected likewise the ontological argument. St. Thomas said that a being than which a greater cannot be conceived is too great to be conceived. His school was more nearly in line with the ancient Stoics who posited a principle of immanent rationality pervading the universe in which man is a participant. Consequently, that on which all men are agreed may be assumed to be true. Since all men believe in God—in that age there were no ' avowed atheists—from universal consent one may infer existence. But by reason one cannot scale the heights of Christian truth. In consequence, faith and knowledge become mutually exclusive. When I say I believe, I mean that I do not know. They are not, however, antithetical. The one leads up to the other. Reason proceeds from nature, from the bottom up. Revelation proceeds from God downwards. They meet and interpenetrate. What revelation proffers, reason can elucidate. There is thus a theological hierarchy with no serious fissures. (*See Reading No. 7, I A.*)

The Nominalists were not able to lay hold of a universal such as God by direct experience or through universal reason, because—since reality consists only of unrelated particulars—all that one can experience is one particular at a time. In their empiricism they resembled Aristotle, though they went beyond him in their inability to put things together. They might argue with Aristotle and with Thomas, who followed him here, that things, even though unrelated, require an ultimate cause, and motion also requires an initial mover. The first cause and the prime mover are God.

But it was when they came to the more specifically Christian tenets that the divergence between the three schools became more acute. The doctrine of the Trinity affords an example.

The Doctrine of the Trinity. The Augustinians undertook to demonstrate the Trinity. The classic example is that of Richard of St. Victor, who argued in Neoplatonic fashion that God is self-diffusive being. From the Father the Son is generated, and from both the Spirit proceeds. But why stop at three? Because God is love and love requires a lover, a beloved and a third to obviate jealousy. The quaintness of the argument should not obscure the nature of the reasoning, which involves really a combination of the Greek view of God as the abyss of dynamic being and the Hebrew picture of God as a person who speaks, commands and loves. Endless diffusion would dissipate the very concept of personality. The significance of this approach lies in the confidence in the possibility of demonstration. One finds it among those who believed in the universal in which man shares and in the capacity of man, even in the flesh, to behold the face of God. And here, of course, knowledge and belief are not divided.

The middle group, following actually on this point in the wake of St. Augustine, said that the Trinity cannot be demonstrated, but can be illustrated. Just as one would not know that tracks in a meadow had been made by a cow if one had never previously seen a cow, so one would not recognize the Trinity in man if one did not know by revelation of the Trinity in God. But knowing that God is triune, one perceives that man, made in His image, is endowed with memory, intellect and will. These are not related after the same manner as the three persons in God, but they enable man to have some inkling of the structure of the Godhead. Here knowledge and faith are exclusive, but not antithetical.

But the Nominalists, since they posited no universals, had no one substance with which to hold the three persons in unity. These persons became in consequence three independent entities, three absolutes, three gods—that is to say, from the philosophical point of view. Nevertheless, we are to believe that God is both three and one because this is taught by theology. This position has been described as "double truth." That it was not. There is only one truth, namely the truth of revelation set forth in theology, but there are two kinds of logic, the philosophical and the theological, which arrive at contradictory conclusions. The philosophical must be rejected. Knowledge and belief, reason and faith have now become antithetical. Faith is blind reliance on that which is given by the Church. This position is called Fideism. It did not become dominant until the fourteenth and fifteenth centuries and marks in some respects the disintegration of scholastic theology.

Frequently, treatises on scholasticism set Scotists and Thomists over against each other, but recent scholarship has diminished the gap between Scotus and Thomas. The significant difference is that Scotus so stressed the absoluteness of the divine will as to leave no ethical precept unamenable to dispensation except the love of God. This position undercuts the concept of natural law, a universally binding moral code.

The Preachers. If one turns from the theologians to the preachers of the Middle Ages, one naturally finds

less abstract ratiocination. The passion of Christ had become a central theme with no little dwelling also on the
fires of hell and the joys of heaven. (*See Reading No. 7,
II.*) But there was also much about the life terrestrial,
though frequently cast in a form so fantastic as to seem
remote from actual life. Some of the manuals for preachers are singularly inept in all of the allegories which they
spin about the unicorn, the phoenix, the pelican and the
like. And then there are many tales of the miraculous
interventions of the Virgin or of some saint. But still the
point which the "bestiaries" enjoined was some precept
of the moral life. And if the devils at times devoted themselves to trivialities such as reporting the times when the
tenor set the pitch too high for the choir, on the whole
they were occupied with first-rate misdemeanors. And if
the Virgin was betimes grossly unfair in snatching from
the devil a soul legitimately forfeit, in the main both she
and all the saints were on the side of those who "did
justly, loved mercy and walked humbly with their God."
Some of the preaching was of a superbly high order. (*See
Reading No. 7, IV.*)

Popular Religion. When we look at popular religion we meet, naturally, with much that was crude. Superstition is rife in all ages. Caesar of Heisterbach in his
Dialog on Miracles (IX, viii), for example, tells of a
woman who to stop her bees from dying secreted a part
of the wafer at the mass in her mouth and placed it in
the hive. Whereupon the insects constructed about it from
their sweetest honeycomb a chapel complete with windows, roof, bell tower, porch and altar on which they
laid the Lord's body and flew around buzzing loudly to
the praise of the Creator. The cult of relics was so rampant that one monk obliged the brethren by cutting off his
beard and giving them the hairs in advance of his demise.
He was deeply hurt that his sanctity was not sufficiently
esteemed to make his whiskers treasurable.

More surprising then superstition is blasphemy. One
would not expect this in an age of faith, but there was
free swearing by the teeth of God, the eyes of God, the
shins of God—God, of course, here meant Christ—and
by the belly of the Virgin. The modern ejaculation
"Zounds" is a corruption of "God's wounds." There were
even parodies on the mass, scandalously funny if one un-

derstands the word play. Take this example: "O Lord, who hast made the multitude of the rustics for the service of the clerics and soldiers, and hast sown discord between us and them, grant unto us whomsoever we may be that we may live from their labors, enjoy their wives and rejoice in their mortifications through our Lord God Bacchus, who swilleth and draineth through the mugs of the mugs. Straw men." (The corresponding words in the mass are: "Christ, who liveth and reigneth through the ages of the ages. Amen.") What is so surprising is that during the Middle Ages no one was burned for blasphemy, presumably because blasphemy, no matter how irreverent, is a form of faith. Blasphemy is not outrageous if that toward which it is directed is not believed. To swear by God's teeth is to confess the incarnation.

Much more disconcerting to the Church and to the individual was the inability to believe. Here there was no irreverence, no denial, but an agonized effort to overcome incapacity. The monk Othloh (b. 1010 A.D.) doubted whether there were any profit in Holy Scripture and whether God were actually almighty. If there were a God, how could there be such confusion in the world about? Prostrate and consumed with bitterness, he cried out, "O thou Omnipotent, if such thou art, and if thou art everywhere, as I have so often read, show me, I beseech thee, who thou art and what thou can't do. Free me right quickly from these besetting perils, for more of these trials I cannot endure." Straightway the cloud was dispelled and the light of knowledge shone in his heart.

But if banalities, irreverence and unbelief are discoverable in popular religion, there was much also among plain folk of a high quality. Take the earliest lullaby in the English tongue and the quatrain "Sunset on Calvary." (*See Reading No. 7, II C.*) In an age when so much of religion consisted in a venal bargaining with God, it is refreshing to read of the woman who carried a chafing dish of live coals and a flask of water in order with the first to burn up paradise and with the second to extinguish hell that men might be good solely for the love of God. And for sensitivity take the story of Marjorie Kempe. Sitting alone in a church before a *pietà,* she was overcome with compassion and wept grievously. Then a priest came to her and said, "Lady, it is a long time now since Jesus has been dead." "Sir," she answered, "his death is as new to me as if he had died this very day, and so I think it ought to be to you and to all Christian people. We ought always to be mindful of his love to us and always think of the bitter death which he died for us."

— 8 —

REALIGNMENTS

The prestige of the papacy appeared to mount after Innocent III, but this was only because the empire declined. In the struggle with the Church, the house of Hohenstaufen was crushed. The last scion was executed in 1268 A.D. One could readily infer that God intended the papacy to fill the gap, and Innocent IV went so far as to affirm that the Church held the two swords. Though actually wielding only the spiritual, she it was who consigned the temporal to rulers to be used at her behest. (*See Reading No. 8, I A; compare B.*)

Yet at the very time that such claims were made, the Church's success was her undoing. Quite perceptibly a new force was rising, the force of nationalism. Spain and England—and especially France—were moving toward consolidation. The papacy had contributed to the process. The first crusade under papal auspices had been an achievement in French unity. The Albigensian crusade had ended in the annexation of Provence to the crown of France. When now a conflict arose with France, the Church could no longer manipulate the empire, now weakened, as a counterpoise.

The quarrel was a revival of the ancient attempt of the crown to lay hands on the goods of the Church. Philip the Fair appealed to the old claims of royal patronage and control. The conflict assumed a new aspect because of the restoration of a monied economy. This made it possible

for the papacy to levy exactions on the local churches
and to draw the money to Rome. It also made possible
direct taxes on these same churches by the crown. The
Church had given the king a certain warrant at this point
by authorizing such taxes to defray crusading expenses.
But when then the Church transferred the crusading idea
back to Europe and applied it to her own efforts against
France, the king preferred to take the money for counter
measures. The upshot was that Philip forbade the exportation of gold to Rome. Pope Boniface VIII replied with
two famous bulls. The first, *Clericis Laicos,* forbade the
king to exact and ecclesiastics to pay such levies on the
Church's income. The second, *Unam Sanctam (see Reading No. 8, II A and B),* declared that every human being,
for salvation, must be subject to the Roman pontiff. This
was a grandiloquent gesture of an effete autocracy, yet
for all its sweeping pretensions somewhat ambiguous.
What did "subject" mean—in spirituals, or also in temporals? Boniface was not as precise as Innocent IV. The outcome was a debacle. The very person of the pope was
attacked by agents of the king. Boniface was summering
at Anagni in the year 1303 A.D. He was maltreated and
shortly thereafter died. Anagni was the reverse of Canossa.

The Babylonian Captivity.   The papacy then moved
from Rome to Avignon on the borders of southern France,
there to remain from 1305 to 1378, a period so nearly
corresponding to the seventy years of the Jews in exile as
to be called the Babylonian Captivity. All the popes were
French. The papacy had lost its international character.
One evidence of the subservience of the Church to the
crown of France was the suppression of the Templars.
They were a monastic military order, immensely wealthy,
armed, subject only to the pope and with nothing to do
because the crusades were over. The last Christian for-
tresses in the Holy Land fell to the unbelievers in 1291
A.D. The king could not but regard the Templars as a
menace to the authority of the crown. The straightforward
procedure would have been simply demobilization, but
that would have been to admit that the crusades were
over, which no one was prepared to acknowledge. Crusading appeals continued to be issued well into the sixteenth
century. Philip hit on the happy device of accusing the

order of heresy. Every member in France was arrested simultaneously. Some of the leaders were tortured and confessed. They were then turned over to the Inquisition. The pope announced that he would hear the case. Thereupon those who had confessed repudiated their confessions. But the Inquisition then treated them as relapsed heretics. Fifty-nine were burned at the stake in Paris, including the Grand Master, Jacques de Molay. The order was suppressed, and the pope acquiesced. This is an example of the use of the Inquisition as an instrument of national policy.

The popes now found themselves in serious financial straits. The papal estates, on the papacy's removal to Avignon, had promptly been overrun by the Italian nobles. The pope's income was cut off. Then it was that Pope John XXII revived and contrived all manner of devices for squeezing money out of the local churches everywhere, but especially in France. There were indulgences. These were originally remissions of penalties imposed for sin, in return for which relaxations the recipient made a contribution. The practice went back to the old Germanic custom of allowing a blood debt to be commuted into a money payment. The indulgence was, however, more than a simple remission of penalty by the pope. It was a transfer of credit from the treasury of the superfluous merits accumulated by Christ and the saints, who were better than they needed to be for their own salvation, and whose extras could be applied to the accounts of others in arrears. (*See Reading No. 8, III C.*)

Services and annates were terms applied respectively to levies of the first year's income on larger and smaller benefices. When a vacancy occurred, the pope filled it by moving a bishop from another see, and so on in a chain reaction; from each he reaped the first fruits. When the pope visited a bishopric his expenses were paid. It proved cheaper to pay him not to come, in which case he could accept simultaneous invitations. Expectations gave one a lien for a fee on a bishopric when it should become vacant. Offices in the papal chancery were multiplied and sold, and there were various fees—for example, for dispensations from marriage regulations. By these and like devices the popes and the cardinals together during the period of the Babylonian Captivity had a larger income than the king of France. Sixty-three per cent of this papal income was spent on wars to recover the lost Italian estates. One cannot but marvel that the kings of France should allow this to be. If the exportation of money was forbidden to Rome, why was it allowed to Avignon? Perhaps the kings felt that a papacy under French control was a sufficient asset in international politics to warrant the expense.

But the trouble was that the papacy without independence soon ceased to be an asset. Should the rivals of France obey a papacy subject to France? There were rumblings of disaffection. England was ready to repudiate altogether the vassalage to the pope incurred by King John. As for the then emperor, Louis of Bavaria, he attacked the Church at the most fundamental point in that he dared on his own authority to declare a divorce to free a certain woman for marriage to his son. This was to invade the domain of the sacraments. The pope replied with excommunication, interdict and deposition, all of which for a long time Louis blithely disregarded. The Protestant schism came close to being anticipated by two hundred years.

Critique of the Pope.   But if John did not have a quarrel with the king of France, he did with the Franciscans in France. The disciples of the *Poverello* were understandably critical of such a financial wizard. John clamped down on some of the Spirituals and when they were recalcitrant, sent them to the stake. But then he made a great tactical blunder when he affirmed, contrary to the pronouncement of his predecessor Nicholas III, that Christ had property. Thereupon both branches of the Franciscans rallied in a united proclamation that the pope was a heretic. To be thus denounced by the omnipresent mendicants was more serious than a rift with the empire. But John had to face a coalition of both. The leaders of the Franciscans fled to the court of Louis. The most prominent among them was William of Ockham, who has already been mentioned as the leader of the Nominalists. William roundly defended the right of the empire to independence in a vein reminiscent of the imperial claims in the investiture controversy. Much more radical was his theory of authority in the Church. Here his Nominalism becomes apparent. He atomized the Church. It is made up, said he, of constitutents, and no one constituent is immune from error. The pope may be wrong, a council may be wrong, the laity may be wrong, all of the men may be wrong and the truth will reside only with women. At least one part will at a given time be right, because Christ said that the gates of hell would not prevail against the Church, but no given part is infallible. (*See Reading No. 9, I A.*) Such a view almost inevitably eventuated in placing authority in the Bible, interpreted individually.

At the court of Louis was also an Italian, by name Marsiglio or Marsilius of Padua. He adapted to the new situation the theory already advanced by Cardinal Ugolini to relieve the Franciscans of their dilemma in accepting alms only for a day. The Church should hold the *dominium* and grant to the Franciscans the *usus*. Marsilius now said that the state should hold the *dominium* and grant to the Church the *usus*. He proposed to reduce the entire body of the clergy to the state of Franciscan poverty and to place the control of all funds into the hands of him whom he called the *legislator,* but whom we should call the executive. (*See Reading No. 9, I B.*) Here was a doctrine which afforded a very convenient pretext for the confiscation of ecclesiastical goods. No wonder that Henry VIII had this tract translated into English.

Plainly, the continued residence of the popes at Avignon was destroying the prestige and universalism of the papacy. Pope Urban VI went back to Rome in 1378 A.D. His cardinals refused to follow and elected another pope. He then created a new body of cardinals and there came thus to be two popes and two bodies of cardinals. This was the beginning of the great papal schism which was not healed until 1417 A.D. All Europe was divided in consequence. The French supported the Avignonese pope and the English, the Roman. The Scotch, through enmity for the English, sided with the French. Flanders and Germany, out of enmity for the French, lined up with England. Spain, after some hesitation, joined France through fear of England. Even more disconcerting were the divisions in the bishoprics, where one who aspired to replace a bishop would announce himself in favor of the opposite pope.

Conciliarism. In an effort to end the schism and prevent its recurrence, a movement arose called Conciliarism. One of its greatest architects was Pierre D'Ailly, a French cardinal, a great theologian and scientist, whose views impelled Columbus to undertake his voyage. D'Ailly, and his colleagues in this school of thought, argued that the seat of authority in Christendom resides not in the papacy, but in councils. They pointed out that councils had been convened in the very earliest days of the Church, for Peter and Paul had attended a council at Antioch (Acts 15). The normal way of settling disputes for a full five hundred years after Constantine had been by councils. They had been summoned not by popes, but by emperors.

The practical problem then was to find a way of assembling a council to end the schism. Each pope and the successors of each pope professed willingness to attend, but each kept proposing a place more remote from the other until the cardinals of both popes in disgust went ahead without either and assembled at Pisa in the year 1409 A.D. The popes at that moment were *Benedictus* and *Gregorius*. The council referred to them as *Benefictus* and *Errorius* and declared them deposed. A new pope was elected as Alexander V. But the other two did not then retire, and instead of two popes there were three. Alexander V died shortly and was replaced by Baldassare Cossa, an ex-pirate, an Italian condottieri, commander of the papal troops, who took the title of John XXIII. There were still three popes.

The failure of Pisa was now explained on the ground that the council had not been summoned by either a pope or an emperor. If this double authority were enlisted, then surely a council would succeed. The emperor at this juncture was Sigismund of Hungary, who was very eager to have his legitimate tenure as Holy Roman Emperor confirmed by the pope, but such coronation would be futile, of course, unless performed by a legitimate pope. He was most open to the suggestion that he call a council. As for John XXIII, all of his military skills had not saved him from being driven out of Rome by the king of Naples. John, too, was willing to join in the issuing of an invitation. The place agreed upon was Constance in Switzerland, where the council was to sit from 1414 to 1418 A.D.

Thither the prelates came up. There were a goodly number of eminent churchmen and a larger number less

eminent and less estimable. John XXIII sought to manipulate the council by the creation of a new batch of Italian
bishops, but he was foiled in that the voting was set up by
nations. The universities were organized according to nations, except that the term applied to smaller units than
today. The university of Prague, for example, had four
nations, the Czech and the Silesian, Bavarian and Saxon,
which today would all be called German. But the nations
at Constance were those to whom the name is still given.
The four were the English, French, German and Italian.
All of John's new bishops were thus lumped together into
one. He tried then to wreck the council by injecting national jealousies, for this was the period of the Hundred
Years' War between England and France, but wars in
those days were not so all-embracing and an Englishman
could travel unmolested through France to attend a
Church council. Cardinal D'Ailly kept the peace and
again frustrated the pope. John XXIII thereupon induced
one of the kinglets to challenge another to a tournament,
and while the council took off a day for the spectacle, the
pope—disguised under a slouch hat and mounted on a
sorry nag—slipped out of Constance. There was conster-
nation. Without the pope could the council proceed, or
would it fail like Pisa? D'Ailly persuaded the council of
its authority as a council and tranquillized the cardinals
by constituting them into a voting unit like the nations.
John was at length caught and brought back to Constance,
where he was accused of enough crimes to hang a cohort,
ranging all the way from incest to an offer to sell the head
of John the Baptist to Florence. He was deposed, despoiled of his Fisherman's ring and incarcerated in a
dungeon. His successor made him a cardinal, and for
centuries he has been sleeping under his cardinal's hat in
the baptistery of Florence, where the guides now have to
explain that as John XXIII he has been stricken from the
list.

The question then was whether first to elect a new pope
or to reform the Church. The council, whose constituency
savored largely of the Church unreformed, decided in
favor of first ending the schism. A new pope was elected,
who took the title of Martin V. Of the other two rivals,
one died and one resigned. The schism was over. The reform of the Church was postponed. The council issued

the decree *Sacrosancta,* affirming the authority of councils, and the decree *Frequens,* which set the intervals at which they should convene. (*See Reading No. 8, IV.*) The council then went home.

Heresy in England and Bohemia. They did one other thing before leaving. An effort was made to extirpate heresy in Bohemia and, less directly, in England. The two countries were closely linked because Richard II of England was married to Anne of Bohemia, and students went back and forth from Oxford to Prague. Heresy began in England. The leader was John Wyclif (1324-1384 A.D.). The turning point in his ecclesiastical career was the year 1378 A.D., the outbreak of the papal schism. Before that he had been an ardent declaimer against papal encroachments upon England. He amplified the thought of Marsilius about *dominium* and *usus.* Lordship, said he, belongs to God and *usus* to man. But if man is guilty of *abusus,* he may be deprived of the *usus.* If the Church is guilty of abuse, she may be despoiled by the state. Wyclif protested particularly against the papal demand that England pay up the feudal dues levied ever since John had made her a fief of the papacy. But when in 1378 A.D. there came to be two popes, each claiming that the other was damned, Wyclif said they were both right.

Wyclif then set forth a number of ideas highly subversive of the papacy. (*See Reading No. 8, V A.*) The most radical was the doctrine that the true Church is the Church of the predestined who can be recognized by a moral test. At any rate, if one cannot be sure that the good are the elect, one may be confident that the bad are the non-elect. And a pope whose conduct is in glaring contrast with that of Christ is a "damned limb of Lucifer." Wyclif, like Ockham and Marsilius, held that all of the clergy should embrace an almost Franciscan type of poverty, this not in imitation of St. Francis, but of Christ. A vivid contrast was drawn between Christ the lowly and the pope the lordly. The pope, since in opposition to Christ, was antichrist, and this in the Middle Ages meant the demonic apocalyptic figure of Antichrist.

Wyclif attacked also the doctrine of the mass as defined at the fourth Lateran council in terms of transsubstantiation. As a philosophical realist he held that substance cannot be annihilated. Therefore, after the words of consecration the substance of bread and wine remain. This was called the doctrine of remanence. Wyclif did not deny the real presence of the body of Christ in the sacrament. This is something added to and existing alongside of the natural elements. This doctrine, called consubstantiation was really not so radical, because it states that a change does take place when the priest pronounces the words *Hoc est corpus meum*. But at any rate the now-orthodox formula of the Church was denied.

Wyclif asserted, as Ockham had done, the authority of the Bible as the ultimate source of Christian truth and sponsored a translation into the vernacular (from which the line runs to the King James and the Revised Standard Version). But although in so many respects Franciscan in his ideas, Wyclif excoriated the friars as no longer fired by their earlier zeal and as encroaching upon the proper role of the parish priest. One notes that in the same period Chaucer's kindliest portrait is that of the parish priest, while he too satirized the friars. Wyclif organized a company of parish priests dedicated to the cure of souls. They came to be called Lollards. Because protected by the crown, Wyclif died in bed. But after his death the act *De Haeretico Comburendo* was directed against his followers, who were so far exterminated that one cannot tell whether a trickle of influence passed from them into the English Reformation.

The ideas of Wyclif had a more persistent influence in Bohemia. Hus (1366-1415 A.D.) was a preacher in the vernacular and a vehement denouncer of the sins of the clergy. (*See Reading No. 8, V B.*) He had the same theme of Christ and Antichrist and drew a vivid picture of the pope on a sumptuously caparisoned war horse driving off the devout with a silver club while Christ the Redeemer, in the form of the Sacred Host, was carried at the head of the procession on a donkey. Hus shared Wyclif's predestinarian theory of the Church. This was really his most radical view. He did not agree with Wyclif that the substance of bread and wine remain after the consecration. Hus was accused of saying that the sacraments performed by an unworthy priest are invalid. Here he made a distinction between the sacramental and the pastoral functions of the priest, the latter of which are emphatically invalidated by an unsavory life, but not the former.

The Hussites. Hus came into conflict with one party after another, first with the Germans at the University of Prague. We have noted that they had three nations and therefore three votes to the Czech one. King Wenzel reversed the proportion and made Hus the rector. The Germans packed and left, to found the University of Leipzig, carrying with them resentment against the Czechs and Hus. He alienated Archbishop Zbynek by endorsing some of the "heresies" of Wyclif. King Wenzel was angered when Hus defended students who burned the bull of indulgence issued by Pope John XXIII to finance his crusade against the king of Naples. Hus went for a time into retirement.

The suggestion was made that he might be brought for a hearing before the Council of Constance. He was delighted with the proposal, supposing that if he defended his views from the Scriptures any learned body of churchmen would concur. The Emperor Sigismund favored the plan. He was brother to Wenzel and his heir, and wished the territories he would inherit purged of heresy. The emperor gave a safe conduct to Hus both to come and to go. When Hus arrived he was shocked by the immorality. The pope had him promptly thrown into a dungeon and Sigismund repudiated the safe conduct when informed that with those who have no faith, the Church is not obligated to keep faith.

Hus was accused of positions which he had never held. When called upon to retract them anyway he replied that he could not recant what he had never taught, for to do so would be to imply that such views had once been his. Then a new point was introduced. His followers had started to give the wine as well as the bread in the mass to the laity. When the matter was brought to Hus' attention, he approved. This was a matter of usage rather than of dogma and the withholding was only a few centuries old, but to reject the current practice was deemed insubordinate. On all points Hus appealed to his conscience. Cardinal D'Ailly told him that he could not be judged on his conscience, but only on the evidence. Hus was condemned not by the worst, but by the best men at Constance. Often enough it is the saints who burn the saints. Only they care enough to die and kill. D'Ailly was trying through the authority of councils to save the Church from disintegration. Hus' doctrine of the Church of the predestined was just as subversive of conciliar as of papal authority. Technically, Hus died for refusing to recant what he had never believed. After the burning, the ground around the stake was dug up lest the Bohemians should be able to scrape up any ashes to take home as relics.

They had no need of relics. Bohemia was aflame. National spirit, resentment against Germans allied with Rome, moral zeal directed against corrupt churchmen whether German, Italian or Czech, a lay spirit demanding that the cup be not withheld from the untonsured—all these kindled armed rebellion. Under the leadership of the blind general Zizka, the more radical among the Hussites swept over Bohemia and even carried the crusade into Saxony.

Conciliarism might have died long since had not the crusading heretics menaced the European peace. The Council of Basel was convened in 1431 A.D. The constitution was more democratic. Any bishop could vote. An attempt was made to split the Hussites, granting communion in both kinds, *i.e.* the chalice as well as the wafer to the laity. This would have satisfied the moderates called Utraquists (from the Latin *uter-utra,* meaning both). But it would not placate the implacables who would have no truck with Rome on any terms. They were dominant, but at length they were defeated on the field of battle. Catholicism was restored in Bohemia, but Hussitism in its more moderate form was not exterminated. Here was an example before the Reformation of the toleration of two faiths in one territory.

The Council of Basel behaved as if it meant never to disband. Actually it was in session from 1431 to 1449 A.D. This cost money, and the council began to infringe on papal finances. Pope Eugenius III resisted. Then most opportunely a way opened for undercutting the council. The Greeks appealed for help against the Turks pressing on Constantinople. It was to fall in 1453 A.D. The Greeks faced the question whether to negotiate with the council or the pope. Eugenius offered them a more convenient place of meeting at Ferrara. Here they convened in 1438 A.D. But the Council of Basel did not disband. Now there were two councils, a conciliar schism. And that spelled the debacle of conciliarism. The upshot of it all was that the

Greeks came to an agreement with the pope, who spelled
out for them the western doctrine of the seven sacraments.
(*See Reading No. 7, I B.*) All of this redounded to papal
glory, which was not greatly diminished when gradually
the news reached the west that the east had repudiated
the concessions made by its emissaries. The aid was incon-
sequential to Constantinople, which succumbed to the infidels. Basel sputtered and elected a counter-pope, Felix V,
but he resigned in 1449 A.D., and in that year the Council
of Basel dispersed. The attempt to make the Church into
a constitutional monarchy had failed. The trend toward
absolutism continued unabated.

In 1450 A.D. the papal throne was mounted by Nicholas V, commonly called the first Renaissance pope, because he founded the Vatican library.

— 9 —

THE CHURCH AND
THE RENAISSANCE

During the age of the Renaissance the papacy had become a cross between a universal monarchy and an Italian
city-state. Pretensions to universalism were not abandoned,
but involvement in Italian politics made the popes appear
little different from the despots of the other Italian city-
states, Florence, Milan, Venice and Naples. For about
fifty years in the late fifteenth century these states maintained a balance of power based on an equality of strength
and a community of culture. But they sparred constantly
for advantage, fought every summer, made as few corpses
and as many prisoners as possible, at the end of the season
counted the chips, paid the score and settled down for
the winter. The popes participated. There was Sixtus IV,
whose nephews assured him that his preeminence required
the elmination of the Medici at Florence. "I will have no

killing," said he. "Holy Father," said they, "when it is done you will forgive." "I will have no killing," he insisted. "Leave it to us," said they. *"Io sono contento,"* said he. With just what he was content is not quite plain. Certainly if he thought the Medici could be eliminated without killing he was naive.

His nephews enlisted the Pazzi, the rival family in Florence, and the Florentine Archbishop Salviati. One of the Pazzi called on Girolamo di Medici and invited him to join in going to mass. As they walked Pazzi affectionately felt Girolamo to see whether he was armed. In the church he stabbed him. Lorenzo di Medici saw, wrapped a cloak around his left arm for a shield, fought off his assailants, leaped into the sacristy, rallied his party and hanged Pazzi and Archbishop Salviati from the Palazzo Publico. The pope protested against such treatment of an Archbishop and was advised that silence would be discreet.

Then there was Julius II, Julius the Titanic. He came at the end of the century when the French were invading Italy and the system of the five states was being disrupted. To expel the French he made a league with other Italian states and for the first time employed Swiss mercenaries, for whom Michelangelo designed the uniform still worn by the Swiss guards in Vatican City. Julius fought also against foes in Italy. At the head of his own troops he laid siege to Bologna and was the first to scale the walls. He was a great patron of the arts. He it was who discovered Bramante, Raphael and Michelangelo, who started to execute for him a magnificent mausoleum for which only the Moses was completed. Julius tore down the rotting basilica of St. Peter, which went back to the time of Constantine, and laid the piers for the present St. Peter's.

Are such popes to be considered Christian? They thought so. Others in their own day did not. Erasmus pictured the soul of Julius arriving at the gate of heaven and demanding admittance from St. Peter, who asked what the pope had done to deserve it. Julius replied that he had made the papacy great. He had captured Bologna. "What for?" inquired Peter. "Was the ruler a tyrant, a heretic?" "O, no!" "Why then?" "I wanted Bologna for my son." "Popes with wives and sons?" "You don't understand. Not wives, but sons." Peter again demands to know what the pope has done and is given an account of the splendors of the papacy. The pope is told that in Peter's day it was not so and is refuted with the retort that in his day the papacy was not worth having. Erasmus never admitted nor expressly denied the authorship of this diatribe. Actually, it is less an accurate picture of Julius II than a composite of Renaissance popes.

Renaissance, Pagan or Christian.   Some say that the Renaissance was pagan and the popes the most pagan of all. Certainly in the whole period there was none distinguished for spirituality. Alexander VI, the Spanish pope Rodrigo Borgia, had introduced the prevalent system of concubinage into the papacy itself. By one concubine he had four illegitimate children, including Lucretia and Caesar Borgia. Leo X was an amiable dilettante who spent more money on gambling than ever was paid to Raphael and Bramante.

What then of the Renaissance? Was it essentially pagan? With regard to any generalizations about the Renaissance one needs to ask: is it true? was it new? was it then held by many or by few? The despots of the Italian Renaissance were undoubtedly as promiscuous as May flies, as cunning as spiders and as remorseless as sharks. But how new was such behavior? One can match it among the Plantagenets. The difference is perhaps that the Sforzas, the Viscontis and the Medici were elegant cut-throats who subsidized arts and letters. The frank description and the unblushing condoning of political unscrupulousness was new in Machiavelli, but how representative? The prevailing thought of his age was in the moral tradition. Witness the *Utopia* of More and the *Institute of the Christian Prince* of Erasmus.

But does not the luxuriant employment of pagan mythology indicate a departure from the Christian faith? If so, what then shall we say of Dante? He has Charon ferrying souls across the Styx, yet would any deny that Dante was a Christian poet? The suggestion has been made that the use of pagan mythology was the successor to the lush allegory of fantastic beasts in the Middle Ages. Both represented an escape from the naked brutalities into the realm of symbol. But one has still to ask why in any case there should have been a shift from allegory to mythology. The answer may be that pagan mythology had become usable precisely because paganism was dead. In the early days of the Church, when paganism was a living rival, the Christian writers were chary of compromising allusions. But during the Renaissance no one thought seriously of reviving paganism. A man who would not say "By Jesus," because he believed in Jesus, would say "By Jove," because he did not believe in Jove.

But are there not pagan elements in the art of the Renaissance? In a measure yes, but one needs to distinguish between the injection of a pagan sentiment into a Christian frame and the use of a pagan frame to convey a Christian sentiment. For example, there is a painting of St. Sebastian with a *bel corpo ignudo* (a fair nude torso), perforated with arrows which in no way mar the composure of his classic beauty. This is pagan. But again one may find a representation of the annunciation in which the angel Gabriel speaks to Mary through a crevice in a partition. What is this if not Pyramis and Thisbe? Yet the whole treatment is as devout as that of Fra Angelico.

Renaissance architecture is often described as of the earth, earthy in comparison with the Gothic. The Renaissance does make use of the dome, which goes back to classical antiquity. The Pantheon may have provided the model for St. Peter's. But the pagan mode as such is not necessarily irreligious. The Gothic reaches for the stars. The Renaissance dome suggests the majesty of marshalled spaces. The dome is the firmament of heaven. Another contrast often made is that in the Gothic the light streams down from above, but in the Renaissance style enters through the windows from below. But this is not altogether true. The Pantheon has an aperture in the center of the dome through which a shaft of light descends, and in St. Peter's to behold a ray of sunlight flash from the throne of God to the high altar engenders a sense of awe and uplift.

Finally, one is told that the Renaissance presents a new view of man. The classic example is the tract by Pico della Mirandola on *The Dignity of Man (see Reading No. 10, I)*, in which he says that man is the modeler and sculptor of his own destiny. The claim is made that here is a new picture of man as the master of his fate. As a matter of fact, there is nothing really new in this concept. What we encounter here is essentially a version of Neoplatonic mysticism. Man stands at the center of the great chain of being with ability either to descend to the level of the brute or to ascend until united with the ineffable One. The same theme is found in the Christian mystics. Take, for example, St. Bonaventura's *Itinerary of the Soul to God*. The main difference is that Pico has drawn also from the language of the ancient mystery religions, from the Christianized Gnosticism of Hermes Trismegistus as well as from pagan mythology. At the same time, there are quotations from Sacred Scripture. The mood is distinctly religious though not specifically Christian, since this type of mysticism has no real need for Christ as the mediator on the ladder of ascents. A further point to remember is that Pico's confidence in man's power to descend or ascend at will is not characteristic of his age, in which many were addicted to astrological determinism.

As for out-and-out skepticism, there was, if anything, less in the Renaissance than in the Middle Ages. The skepticism which we do find in the Renaissance is medieval in character. But really it was not so much skepticism as fideism. One variety we have already seen, that of Ockham and the Modernists with reference to the Trinity. On the basis of their philosophy the doctrine was untenable, but nevertheless to be believed on the basis of the authority of the Church. Another variety stemmed from the Averroistic tradition, for Averroes, the Arab, interpreted Aristotle to mean that the individual soul is absorbed at death into the world soul, and thus there is no personal immortality. Pursuing this line, Pomponazzi explored, with more acumen than anyone hitherto, the mind-body problem. He concluded that nothing in human experience warrants the assumption that the soul can continue its conscious life after the dissolution of the body. Nevertheless, Pomponazzi did not deny immortality, any more than Ockham denied the Trinity. He, too, was prepared to accept this Christian tenet on the basis of revelation. (*See Reading No. 9, II.*)

Revolt against the Church there was none. The reason may have been that the Church was too lax to be worth revolting against. At any rate, the popes were so far the patrons of the new movements that no need was felt—in Italy, at any rate—for any vehement opposition. Satire we find in plenty. Witness the skit on relics by Boccaccio and the burlesque on the Inquisition by Crotus Rubeanus. (*See Reading No. 10, IV B.*) But this sort of thing was no more indicative of fundamental rebellion than was medieval buffoonery. Boccaccio did not live long enough for us to know how he would have reacted to the Protestant Reformation, but Crotus did, and he remained with the old Church.

Newness in the Renaissance. Nevertheless, it would be a mistake to give the impression that nothing was new and nothing subversive in this period. One element distinctly new was the rise of historical criticism. The great figure here is Lorenzo Valla. By very acute philology and historical analysis he demonstrated that the *Donation of Constantine* could not have originated in the days of Constantine. For one thing, it contained a reference to the image controversy of the eighth century. Mention was made also of satraps who were not officials in Constantine's bureaucracy. Even more, no writer of Constantine's time or for several centuries thereafter ever made mention of this donation. Nor is there any evidence that the popes in the early Middle Ages actually exercised the power said to have been conferred upon them. By a like acumen Lorenzo discredited the legend that Christ had sent a letter to King Abgar of Edessa, together with a portrait of himself painted by Luke the evangelist. A further development of the legend was that when copies of this portrait multiplied the pope was called upon to decide which was the true, the *veron icon* (whence the name of St. Veronica, who was reputed to have handed Christ on the way to the cross a napkin which he pressed to his face, leaving on it the image of his blood-stained features). Finally Lorenzo demolished the legend that the twelve apostles delivered the Apostles' Creed article by article, one for each. (*See Reading No. 10, III.*) Documents on which rested some of the claims of the Church were thus undercut. Of course, papal claims did not cease in consequence and have subsequently been modified in the political sphere, less by reason of the removal of these props than because of clashes with the consolidated national states. At the same time, the exposure of the spuriousness of these documents was used for polemical purposes by the Protestant reformers.

The greatest change as to religion in the age of the Renaissance was a tendency to mute the distinctiveness of Christianity and to take a more tolerant view of other faiths, particularly Judaism and Islam. This is the period in which Boccaccio applied the old story of the three rings to the three faiths. The tale was that a father before his death gave to each of three sons a ring, telling him that by this token he might claim the entire inheritance. When the father died each of the three sons produced an identical ring. Now, these three rings, said Boccaccio, are the three faiths. The story was used again in the age of the Enlightenment by Lessing in his *Nathan the Wise*. Nicolas of Cusa imagined a world parliament of religions in which a common core was formulated as the basis for a common religious observance. (*See Reading No. 10, II A.*) Thomas More posited in *Utopia* a temple in whose central nave all faiths could worship together, while adjoining chapels would provide for diversity. (*See Reading No. 10, II B.*) Erasmus inveighed against the multiplication of dogmas and their enforcement by the arm of the state, seeing that no faith can be true and pleasing to God which is constrained. (*See Reading No. 10, 2 C.*)

There were a number of ways in which Christianity could be accommodated to other religions. One was by discovering in them Christian truths. This Pico did because in the occult lore of the Orient, in the tradition of Pythagorean number symbolism, he could find the doctrine of the Trinity. Another way was to remove from Christianity that which was not to be found in other religions. Early in the sixteenth century the Spaniard Michael Servetus felt that the great obstacle to the willing conversion of the Moors and the Jews was the doctrine of the Trinity. If only this could be removed, surely they would gladly embrace the true faith. What was his relief to discover that the technical terminology of the doctrine of the Trinity is not to be found in the New Testament! He felt then quite free to reject it.

Still a further way was to allegorize the mythologies of all religions until they came to mean the same thing. What they came then to mean was the Neoplatonic scheme of ascent until unified with the ultimate godhead. For the Christian who applied this methodology to his own faith, the birth, the death and the resurrection of Christ became an allegory of similar experience in the life of the soul. This treatment is a deviation from original Christianity, which is anchored on a deed of God in history when

Eternity impinged upon time and the Creator of the World took flesh and dwelt among us. Here was an event unique in time and not a universal interior experience, however much it might prompt and aid such. The proponent of this allegorical approach in the sixteenth century was Sebastian Franck.

There were in the Renaissance, then, subversive tendencies and at the same time much that could be appropriated by Christianity and the Church. The period was marked by a great burgeoning of creative activity in arts and letters, and in the same chronological period there were movements of religious vitality.

— 10 —

PREMONITIONS OF REFORM

The late fifteenth century is frequently viewed in comparison with the sixteenth as a period of decadence and corruption, distinctly in need of the reformatory movements which followed. This judgment invites critical scrutiny. Were the late Middle Ages any more in need of reform than the high Middle Ages? One recalls that in the heydey of the Middle Ages the state of the Church was far from irreproachable. Foulque de Neuilly, preaching before Richard Coeur de Lion, told him to marry off his three shameless daughters. "You lie," snapped the king. "You know I have no daughters." "Yes," said the preacher, "Pride, Avarice and Sensuality." Turning to his courtiers the king retorted, "I call you to witness that I give my daughter Pride to the Templars, my daughter Avarice to the Cistercians and my daughter Sensuality to the prelates." And this was in the pristine days of the Cistercians, when the Templars were the defenders of the Holy Sepulchre and the prelates were sweeping toward the peak of their power. Was there ever a time when the

Church did not need reform? And was there ever a reform save where corruption had not extinguished the resolve to destroy it?

Yet there were certainly some respects in which the situation in the late Middle Ages marked a decline. One was very obviously the prevalence of clerical concubinage. This was itself the outcome of a reform, the attempt to enforce clerical celibacy. All over Europe abuses ensued. Reformers of all stripes were agreed that the corruption was real and rueful. They differed only as to how it should be corrected. The bishop of Constance in 1521 despaired of anything more effective than to raise the tax on priests' children from four to five gulden. Erasmus endorsed and the Protestants introduced clerical marriage. Catholic reformers like Ximenes and the Tridentines eradicated concubinage by drastic discipline.

Pluralism was notoriously rife in every country. Frequent were the complaints about provisions by which the pope "provided" bishops for vacant sees by assigning to them his favorites, largely Italians, whatever the country. These appointees seldom resided in their cures and spent their revenues on anything but their parishes. The system, to be sure, was not wholly bad and sometimes was the equivalent of a modern foundation giving educational fellowships. (*See Reading No. 8, III A.*) Yet in the main they represented exploitation. England tried to stop them by the Statute of Provisors. (*See Reading No. 8, III B.*)

Indulgences became even more rampant when their scope was extended by Sixtus IV to purgatory so that tear-wringing appeals could be addressed to the living to contribute of their abundance to rescue relatives from centuries of woe. The usual arrangement was that the pope received one-third of the yield and the locality two-thirds, but early in the sixteenth century the ratio was stepped up to fifty-fifty. This device, and many another instituted by John XXII, bore with especial weight on Germany because of the lack of a consolidated government to resist papal encroachments. But if one be tempted to paint a picture wholly black, it is refreshing to read the petition of a hermit to the Commons that he might be permitted to expend his own labor in order to build a beacon at the mouth of the Humber. (*See Reading No. 8, III D.*)

Superstition among the people was rife. This we have already noted, and even the more enlightened clergy did little to correct it. One of the indictments to be brought against the clergy in the Middle Ages is not that they were all ignorant. Some were amazingly versed in Scripture (*see Reading No. 7, III*), not to mention theology, but they had developed a technical jargon which the masses did not and were not expected to understand. Theology was almost the pastime of an esoteric clique. As for the ordinary clergy, their learning was manifestly minimal. Many could not locate the Ten Commandments or the Lord's Prayer in Scripture. At the same time, one may wonder whether the episcopal visitations set a sound standard for clerical instruction. Learning was taken to mean the ability to parse Latin. The story is told, for example, of a priest who was asked what, in the invocation in the mass *Te igitur clementisse Pater,* governed *te.* "Why *Pater,*" said he, "because the Father governs everything." Bad Latin, good theology! He was marked down as *sufficienter illiteratus,* but he may not have been such a poor shepherd of souls. One of the greatest reasons for the lack of learning on the part of the clergy was the lack of the printing press. The Renaissance remedied that.

As for monasticism in the late Middle Ages, England has been minutely examined in order to explain why Henry VIII was able to achieve such a comparatively bloodless revolution in the suppression of the monastic houses. Many of the modern apologists for the monks concede a decline and attribute it to the Black Death in 1348 A.D. when the clergy, through fidelity to nursing, lost more heavily than the laity. The population was so reduced after the pestilence that there were not enough worthy recruits to staff the monasteries. To this it may be replied that the number of those in the cowl continued to grow until the time of Henry VII; since the clerics, both secular and regular, are estimated to have been about one in fifty in the population, there was certainly no dearth of personnel.

As for immorality in these monasteries, there has been much debate as to its prevalence. An historian sympathetic to the monks, and unimpeachable as to accuracy, declares that between 1350 and 1450 A.D. the visitations disclose 20 instances in which a superior ought to have been removed, but only 3 were. Yet this same author indicates that the main crime of the monasteries between Chaucer and Henry VIII was not debauchery, but a decent mediocrity. There were no outstanding scholars and no manifest saints.

In the meantime, several reformatory movements were under way in the period called the Renaissance between 1300 and 1500 A.D. One was the great mystical wave among the German Dominicans. Eckhart, one of its most extreme proponents, was a contemporary of John XXII, standing in the tradition of Dionysius the Areopagite. Eckhart found the essence of religion in abstraction from all that is of the senses, all that is concrete and describable, until one is absorbed in the cloud of unknowing. Some of his utterances have a pantheistic ring and came under condemnation. (*See Reading No. 9, III A.*)

Tauler, whose life fell also in the period of the Babylonian Captivity, belonged to a group in the Rhine valley called the Friends of God. Mysticism may have flourished in this area and at this time because of the interdict imposed on the Emperor Louis of Bavaria. To deprive the laity of the sacraments is a dangerous weapon, because they may discover that they can do without them through finding an unmediated access to God. The Friends were only an informal fellowship, certainly not a monastic order. The disciples of Tauler, after his death, continued to compose sermons in his vein and to publish them under his name. In these meditations one finds an emphasis upon love as the core of the Christian religion. God rewards only out of love. God rewards only love and God rewards only with love. (*See Reading No. 9, III B.*) This type of religion was reformatory only by implication. The mystics were not aggressive enough to be reformers vehemently attacking abuses. But the abstraction from the sensory in Eckhart might render the ceremonies and the sacraments of the Church superfluous, and the emphasis of the school of Tauler on love as that alone which God rewards would undercut the whole spirit of indulgences with their transfers of credits.

Another school arose in the Netherlands called The Brethren of the Common Life. They were a quasi-monastic order who lived in community at Deventer, but without taking life-long vows, except that one branch was eventually persuaded to adopt the rule of St. Augustine. Part of their strategy was to plant brothers in schools all over Europe. One of them in Paris was to be the teacher of both Calvin and Loyola, though not at the same time. Their piety found its most perfect expression in *The Imitation of Christ* commonly ascribed to Thomas à Kempis. The emphasis here is on piety rather than intellection. One senses a polemic against scholasticism. This is not true of Eckhart and Tauler, who were both in their theology disciples of Thomas. But the *Imitatio* insists that the Trinity is better pleased by adoration than by speculation. The way of the Christian is to follow Christ in his suffering and to overflow with love to God and all creatures. Strictly speaking, this is not mysticism because there is nothing about absorption into the divine. Yet the emphasis here would certainly diminish interest in scholastic refinements. This movement, like the preceding, depreciated the externals of religion. (*See Reading No. 9, III C.*)

Two Types of Reform. Coincidentally, two types of reform were taking shape which carried over into the next century. They were then to clash with each other and both of them with the Protestant Reformation. One is disposed to wonder whether the variant reforms were not more violent against each other than against that which they sought to correct. This was of course primarily because they were not agreed as to what needed to be corrected. The one variety of these two Catholic reforms stressed rectitude in doctrine and rigor in life. Orthodoxy and discipline were the watchwords.

Among its proponents were two Spaniards, Torquemada and Ximenes. The former was resolved to make Spain a nation solidified by the faith. Spain had been in the earlier Middle Ages the bridge between Christendom and Islam. The crusades terminated this period of co-existence. Spain aligned herself with Christendom. Then came the problem of the Jews. Under pressure, for the first and only time many apostasized and thereby became full Spaniards with the right to marry Christians and to occupy the highest offices in Church and state. But many continued to observe Jewish religious customs in secret. To root out such practices Torquemada succeeded in introducing the Inquisition in 1482 A.D. against the wishes of the loose Spanish pope, Rodrigo Borgia, Alexander

VI, who was himself now more nearly the bridge between Christendom and Islam, for he did not disdain an alliance with the Turks. Backed by the holy zeal of Isabella and the cupidity of Ferdinand, who desired to confiscate the goods of heretics, the Inquisition was introduced. Converted Jews were intimidated into the abandonment of all Jewish practices. Unconverted Jews were banished. Then Granada fell and the same process was applied to the Moors. Not so much the method as the spirit of the rigid orthodoxy of Torquemada was transmitted to the Catholic Reformation in the sixteenth century.

After Torquemada came Ximenes, an amazing figure. He had a letter of expectation on the see of Toledo. The bishop, who regarded such letters as an abuse, would not honor it. Though imprisoned, Ximenes held out till he obtained his desire, then suddenly renounced all preferment to become a strict Franciscan. By a ruse he was induced to leave his cell and became Isabella's confessor. She expanded her confessions to include affairs of state and soon encumbered him with offices. Made the general of the Franciscans, he imposed poverty and celibacy on the friars. Made the Archbishop of Toledo and primate of Castile, and by and by a cardinal as well, he reformed likewise the secular clergy. Poor as a Franciscan, he was rich as an archbishop. He used his wealth to convert the Moors and then to finance a crusade across the straits which he accompanied in person. Yet this man, a rigorous Franciscan, a crusader and a statesman, was also a humanist scholar, dedicated to the new learning in the ancient tongues. He founded the University of Alcala with chairs in Greek and Hebrew and published the *Complutensian Polyglot,* the first edition of the entire Bible, both the Old and the New Testament, in the Hebrew and the Greek. This was in 1522 A.D. Here one finds zeal for orthodoxy and purity conjoined with a dedication to scholarship. These elements also appeared in the Catholic Reformation.

The other type of reform was liberal as to dogma. Erasmus was its prophet, but there were distinguished representatives in all the lands of Europe. In the early years of the sixteenth century there was an interlude of tolerance between the *autos-da-fé* and the fires kindled against the Protestants. Europe and the Church felt secure. The Jews and the Moors were in hand. The medieval sects had been crushed. One could speak more critically without being suspected of incipient defection. England, France, Spain, Germany and even Poland had exemplars of the movement which can be called "evangelical" because it desired to return to the evangelists. There were strains of the Franciscan devotion to the *Poverello*. One very distinct root was the piety of the Brethren of the Common Life among whom Erasmus had been reared. Theological speculation was discouraged as unnecessary and even as inimical to the Christian faith. One of the Brethren pointed out with how little theology the thief on the cross had been saved. The penitent thief became the patron saint of these evangelicals. They developed the theme that he had not been baptised, had not gone to mass, knew nothing of the Trinity or transubstantiation. Only this he knew: that Christ could get him to Paradise. Here is the notion of a minimal theology, simple, intelligible to the meanest intellect, for one need only believe that God is a loving heavenly Father, Christ a divine teacher, and that the whole duty of man is to follow him in meekness and bearing of the cross.

Another strain in this piety was the Neoplatonic disparagement of the carnal, the external as a medium for the communication of the divine. Hence a polemic against relics, pilgrimages, indulgences, fasts and monastic vows on the ground that all of these are outward and nothing matters save the devotion of the heart. The way to persuade men of this is by education. Therefore Erasmus dedicated himself to a lifetime of editing the texts of Christian antiquity. He first brought out in print the New Testament in Greek in 1516 A.D., thus anticipating Ximenes, whose priority applied only to the whole Bible. The program of Erasmus called for peace in the world and in the Church. Therefore he decried war and deplored schism. He was really looking backwards with a wistful nostalgia for the already vanishing unities of Europe.

Many men were optimistic in the early decades of the sixteenth century that reform would succeed through enlightment. Ulrich von Hutten was warbling that this was a great day in which to be alive. Others looked ruefully upon the abuses in the Church and, like Sebastian Brant, taught that St. Peter's bark was about to founder. (*See*

Reading No. 10, V A.) Gailer of Kaisersberg, preaching before the emperor, thought that a new prophet would arise to cleanse the stable. Gailer would not live to see it. (*See Reading No. 10, V B.*) Had he lived he would have had to decide whether his prophet was Martin Luther or Ignatius Loyola.

Much in the religion of the Middle Ages was crude. Folk oscillated between unbridled excesses and penitential orgies. Achievement never tallied with desire. Yet we, who live in a more sophisticated age, find an inescapable charm in the quaint imagery of our simpler forebears. Who today would weave so fair a fancy as that a monk should hang his cloak upon a sunbeam? What discernment lies in the tale of St. Martin, who when confronted by the devil in the guise of Christ the resplendent, eyed him and asked, "Where are the nail prints?" And what indefinable feelings are stirred by the portrayal in a stained-glass window of the Creator wrapped in profound meditation when confronted by the decision to separate light from darkness and counting on His fingers how many days He has left in which to complete the creation!

Part II

READINGS

The translations, when not otherwise indicated, are by the author. Among the sources, the word Mirbt refers to Carl Mirbt, *Quellen zur Geschichte des Papstums,* 4th ed. (Tübingen, 1924).

— Reading No. 1 —

THE EARLY MIDDLE AGES

I. The Barbarian Invasions

Passages from St. Jerome: Ep. 123, 15, CSEL *LVI, 91;* Comment. in Ezechieliem, P.L. *25, pp. 15, 75, and 199.*

✔   ✔   ✔

Innumerable and most ferocious people have overrun the whole of Gaul. The entire area bounded by the Alps, the Pyrenees, the ocean and the Rhine is occupied by the Quadi, Vandals, Sarmatians, Alanni, Gepides, Saxons, Burgundians, Alammani—oh weep for the empire—and the hostile Pannonians. . . . Mainz, once a noble city, is captured and razed, and thousands have been massacred in the church. Worms has succumbed to a long siege. Rheims, the impregnable, Amiens, Artois . . . Tours, Nimes and Strasburg are in the hands of the Germans. The provinces of Aquitaine, of the land of the nine peoples, of Lyons and Narbonne are completely occupied and devastated either by the sword from without or famine within. I cannot mention Toulouse without tears, for until now it has been spared, due to the merits of its saintly bishop Exuperus. The Spaniards tremble, expecting daily the invasion and recalling the horrors of the incursion of the Cimbri. What others are going through the Spaniards suffer in continual anticipation.

. . .

O virgin of Christ, Eustochium, having finished the commentary on Isaiah I had wished to turn to the one on Ezechiel, which I had often promised in memory of your mother Paula, when suddenly word came of the fall of Rome and of the deaths of many of the brethren. I was utterly undone and for days and nights could think of nothing else but of the safety of all. Between hope and desperation I was crucified for the crosses of others. Truly, when the resplendent light of all the earth is extinguished, the head of the Roman empire is severed. Of a truth one may say that in a single city the whole world has perished. "My heart throbbeth within me and a fire burns in my bones." (Psalm 38) . . .

Who would believe that Rome, victor over all the world, would fall, that she would be to her people both the womb and the tomb. Once all the East, Egypt and Africa acknowledged her sway and were counted among her men servants and her maid servants. Who would believe that holy Bethlehem would receive as beggars nobles, both men and women, once abounding in riches? Where we cannot help we mourn and mingle with theirs our tears. . . .

I confess that I promised the commentary on Ezekiel long ago, but I am so involved with the refugees that I have been unable to finish it. There is not an hour, not even a moment, when we are not occupied with crowds of the brethren, when the peace of the monastery is not invaded by a horde of guests so that we shall either have to shut the gates or neglect the Scriptures for which the gates were opened. Consequently I have to snatch furtively the hours of the night, which now with winter approaching are growing longer, and try to dictate by candle light and thus through the labor of exegesis relieve a mind distraught. I am not boasting of our hospitality, as some may suspect, but simply explaining to you the delay.

II. Benedictine Monasticism

A. The Rule of St. Benedict. Selected portions. P.L. 66. The numbers refer to the sections of the Rule.

2) The abbot shall remember that he acts in the place of Christ, of whom Paul was speaking when he said, "We cry Abba, Father." In dealing with the brethren he shall take account of circumstance, mingling encouragement with reproof, the severity of a master and the kindly affection of a father.

3) In matters of great import he shall gather the entire community, taking counsel with the brethren and listening even to the youngest, but let none obstinately defend his opinion.

4) The brethren are enjoined to castigate the body, clothe the naked, visit the sick, bury the dead, console the disspirited, to love their enemies, eschew undue sleep and raucous laughter, to be instant in prayer, to obey in all things the abbot and not to wish to be called holy before being so.

7) [*Then follows an account of the seven steps of humility.*] The seventh step is that one should not only confess to being lower and viler than all but should really believe it. [*The next section deals with the division of the day into periods and of the saying of the holy office.*]

18) Monks are tepid who do not say through the entire psalter and the ordinary canticles every week. Monks shall sleep preferably in a common dormitory, in separate beds, a candle always burning, with the young monks sandwiched between the old and with no knives, lest some one get hurt.

24) An excommunicated brother is to be excluded from the table and the choir.

27) The abbot, as a wise physician, shall send some of the older and wiser brethren to console the offender and provoke him to humility lest he be consumed by overmuch grief.

28) But if he is obdurate he is to be corrected by stripes.

31) The cellarer shall be mature, sober, abstemious, not quarrelsome or insolent, not dilatory or wasteful.

33) No monk shall possess anything of his own, neither book, tablets, stylus, nothing whatsoever, for all things are to be in common.

35) The brethren shall take turns in the kitchen, and

no one is to be excused save for health. At the end of the week he shall clear up everything and wash the towels on which the brethren wash their hands and feet.

39) A choice of two cooked dishes suffices at all times of the year. Fruit and vegetables may be added. A pound of bread for each day is enough, though the abbot may allow an increase to those engaged in hard labor. A pint of wine a day is sufficient, but if more be granted let it be sparingly.

42) After compline the brethren are to be silent while one may read, but not from the Book of Kings in the Old Testament, for this portion of Scripture is not profitable to weak intellects at that hour.

48) Idleness being an enemy of the soul, the brethren shall at certain times be engaged in manual labor, and at other times in reading.

55) By way of bedding, a mattress, blanket, quilt and pillow are adequate. The beds shall be frequently searched by the abbot to detect any hoarding. That there may be no excuse for it each brother shall be allowed a cowl, tunic, shoes, stockings, girdle, knife, stylus, needle, handkerchief and tablets.

57) Craftsmen shall perform their arts with humility, and if any gloats over his skill he shall be transferred to another.

58) A novice received into the order shall in the presence of all and before God and the saints, promise to observe stability, amendment of life and obedience.

62) A brother may be a priest, but let him not on that account be haughty.

64) The abbot is to be elected by the whole community. Let him study to be loved rather than feared. Let him not be distraught and anxious, not too exacting or obstinate, not too zealous or over-suspicious, for then he will never have peace.

66) The porter is to be a wise old man, who knows how to receive and give an answer, whose age will keep him from wandering away. The monastery shall if possible have within it all the necessities: water, mill, garden, bakery and work shops, so that the monks will have no occasion to go abroad, which is not good for their souls.

B. *The Monastic Ideal, from "The Conferences of Cassian,"* Christian Classics *XII, ed. Owen Chadwick (The*

Westminster Press, 1958), pp. 226-227. Conf. 9, sections 25-27.

✓   ✓   ✓

The Lord's Prayer carries one to the higher state of prayer, to that spark-like and ineffable prayer which very few men know by experience. It transcends the senses, is marked by no vocal expression, whether silent or aloud; but the mind, illuminated by an outflowing light from heaven, does not define it in the narrow limit of human language. With the senses unified, it pours forth prayers, almost with violence, as a spring pours forth fresh water, and in a second's time darts up a prayer of such richness that afterwards the mind, returned to normality, cannot easily describe it. . . . Sometimes the spark in the mind is struck by the voice of the cantor, by the counsel of some holy man, by the death of a brother monk. . . . Sometimes it happens because the soul is filled with an indescribable joy and cannot help breaking out into ejaculations, and even the occupant of the next cell feels the power of the happiness in the heart. Sometimes the mind withdraws into a kind of secret abyss of silence, sudden illumination leaves it speechless, the awestruck spirit locks its feelings within or loses feeling altogether, and pours out its longings to God in groanings that cannot be uttered. Sometimes a compunction of grief overwhelms it, and the only way to express it is by a release of tears.

C. The Allure of the Cell. St. Alcuin's lament. Poetae Latini Medii Aevi, *1, ed. Dümmler, No. XXIII, p. 243.*

✓   ✓   ✓

Farewell my cell, forever now farewell,
My sweet abode, my dwelling place beloved.
About thee as a rampart whisper trees,
Their branches richly laden with their bloom.
Ever will thy meadows spring with herbs
Sought by the doctor for his healing art.
Around thee flow the streams through blossomed banks.
Here tends his nets the fisher jubilant.
Fragrant thy wall from apple bearing boughs,
Where white the lily blooms amid the rose.
Warbling all the varied birds sing Lauds

In praise of Him who maketh earth and heaven.
In thee was one time heard the master's voice
Transmitting with his mouth the sacred lore.
In thee at stated times the holy hours
By tongues were chanted and by hearts at peace.

III. The First Medieval Pope, Gregory I

A. The Pope as pastor. Excerpts from the Regula Pastoralis, P.L. 77, pp. 25, 75, 77-78, 89.

The conduct of a prelate should so far excel that of the people as a shepherd is superior to the sheep. He must studiously consider the need for rectitude which lies upon him if the people are properly to be called his flock. He must be pure in thought, prompt in action, discreet in silence, helpful in speech, compassionate towards individuals, preeminent in contemplation, a companion through humility with those who do well, a foe through justice to those who do ill, not negligent of the outward by reason of preoccupation with the inward, nor lax as to the inward because immersed in the outward. . . .

On how to admonish the meek and the hot-tempered:
—Differently are to be admonished the meek and differently the hot-tempered, for sometimes the meek in the exercise of authority suffer from torpor and indolence and through too great inclination to leniency relax unduly the rigor of severity, whereas on the other hand the hot-tempered, when placed in office, become frenzied with anger and harass the life of their subjects by dissipating all quietude of spirit.

On how to admonish the humble and the haughty:—
The humble are to be admonished in one way and the haughty in another. Let the humble hear how eternal are the things for which they yearn, how ephemeral those which they despise. . . . Let the haughty know how ephemeral are the things they seek, how eternal those they forfeit.

On how to admonish the contentious and the irenic:—
In one manner the contentious are to be admonished and in another the irenic. Let the contentious consider the word of the psalmist (Ps. 150:4), "Praise him with timbrel and chorus." Now the timbrel gives the noise of a

dried and stretched hide, but the chorus calls for a harmony of voices. He who castigates his body and deserts the brethren may indeed praise God on the timbrel, but not in the chorus. On the other hand the irenic are not to be so enamored of their present peace as to forget the eternal, for did not David say, "Do I not hate them, oh Lord, that hate Thee?"? (Ps. 138:21-22).

B. The Pope as Administrator. Ep. Lib. *I, ep. XLIV.* P.L. *77, pp. 498-508, condensed.*

1   1   1

We have learned that the workers on the estates of the Church are seriously wronged in that the amount required of them is not observed in times of plenty. We desire that the amount be kept in relation to the market price, be it more or less. Moreover, we consider it to be thoroughly unjust that the peasants of the Church be required to give a larger measure than that in use in the granaries of the Church. We wish you, above all else, to see to it that unjust weights are not used in collecting revenues. If you find any false weights, smash them and make new ones. Particularly we know that the first collection of the tax grievously squeezes our peasants, because they have to pay before harvest and are compelled therefore to borrow from professional moneylenders at usurious rates. Therefore by this admonition we decree that what they would have had to borrow from others be supplied them through Your Experience from the funds of the Church, to be repaid little by little, as the peasants are able. Again we hear that immoderate marriage fees are being charged to the peasants. Therefore we rule that the fee shall not exceed one solidus. We understand that when some supervisors of the estates die their heirs are not allowed to succeed them, but their properties are distrained to the Church. Wherefore we decree that the heirs should succeed. We thank Your Solicitude that, having been told to send our brother his money back, you have consigned the matter to oblivion as if ordered by the least of your slaves. Now, may your Negligence—I will not say your Experience—get this done at once. Felix, the manager of an estate, was to have been exempt from a levy of the Church, but Maximus, the sub-deacon, extracted from him so much that he had to sell or pledge everything he held in Sicily. And now he has been drowned. We command you to redeem whatever he sold or pledged and to take care of his wife and children. See that you do all of this at once. I am absolved in what I have written to you about doing justice. If you neglect, you are guilty. Think of the terrible Judge, who is coming. Let your conscience tremble before He comes, lest you have good reason then to fear when heaven and earth tremble before Him. You have heard what I want. See that you do it.

C. The Pope as Theologian.
1. The doctrine of purgatory. Dial. IV, 39. P.L. 77, p. 396.

✔   ✔   ✔

Although this passage (1 Cor. 3:12) may be understood of the tribulation by fire in this life, nevertheless if any one wishes to understand it as purgation by fire in the life to come, let him observe that the passage says that we may be saved "so as by fire" not with reference to those who build upon iron, brass and lead—that is, the major sins which are harder and less consumable—but rather on wood, hay and straw—that is, the very lightest sins which the fire easily devours. And this, too, is to be borne in mind, that even with regard to the least, there will be no purgation unless one has performed good deeds in this life.

2. The Mass. Dial. IV, 58. P.L. 77, p. 425.

✔   ✔   ✔

Daily in this present life we must immolate the host of his body and blood. For this victim alone saves the soul from eternal death and for us repairs death through the mystery of the Only Begotten, who though death has no more dominion over him, since in himself he is immortal and incorruptible, nevertheless for us is immolated afresh in this mystery of the sacred oblation. Here his body is taken. Here his flesh is distributed to the people. His blood is now poured not into the hands of the infidels but into the mouths of the faithful. Let us consider then what is this sacrifice on our behalf which for our absolution forever imitates the passion of the only begotten Son.

Who, then, of the faithful can doubt that in the hour of this immolation at the voice of the priest the heavens are opened? In this mystery of Jesus Christ the chorus of angels is present, the lowest is united with the highest, the earthly with the heavenly, and the visible with the invisible is made one.

— Reading No. 2 —

THE CONVERSION OF EUROPE

I. Ireland

The Call of St. Patrick. Translated from Libri Epistolarum Sancti Patrici, *ed. Ludwig Bieler (1952)*, Irish Manuscripts Commission.

✓   ✓   ✓

I Patrick, a most unlearned sinner, least of all the faithful and most contemptible among many, had as my father Calpurnius, a deacon, son of the priest Potitus of the village of—. Nearby he had a villa where I was captured. I was about sixteen years old. I did not know the true God and was taken away to Ireland with many thousand men. We deserved it because we had fallen away from God and had not kept His commandments nor obeyed His priests. . . . And God sent His wrath upon us and dispersed us among the nations and to the very ends of the earth. There God opened the sense of my unbelief. Late I deplored my sins and turned with a whole heart to the Lord my God.

After coming to Ireland, daily I tended sheep and often prayed. More and more the love of God was kindled and the fear of God and faith increased. The spirit was at work. By day I prayed a hundred prayers and as many at night. I stayed in the woods and on the mountain. Before dawn I arose and prayed in snow and ice and rain. No

evil did I think and there was no sloth in me, as I now
see, for the spirit was fervent within me. Now it happened that one night in a dream I heard a voice saying
to me, "You do well to fast. Soon you will return to your
fatherland," and again, "See your ship is ready." It was
not close, but about two hundred miles distant and I had
never been there and knew no one. I escaped and left the
man whom I had served six years and by the power of
God, who guided my way, I feared nothing and came to
the ship. But the captain rebuffed me. I turned away and
prayed and before I had finished I heard one of them
calling to me, "Come at once." Immediately I returned
and they said, "Come, we take you on faith." My hope
was to convert them to the faith of Jesus Christ, for they
were pagans.

We set sail and after three days came to land. Then we
travelled twenty-eight days through deserted country.
Food gave out and hunger overtook us. Then the captain
said, "How about it, Christian? You say your God is great
and all powerful. Why don't you pray for us?" I did and
a drove of swine appeared before our eyes. The men killed
many and stayed there two nights. They were revived and
their dogs filled, for many of them were half starved and
dying. These pagans then gave great thanks to God and
held me in high esteem and from then on they had food
in abundance. They also found some honey, and offered
me some, saying it was a sacrifice. Thank God I didn't
touch it. During the night I heard a divine voice saying,
"Two months and you will be with them [*that is, with his
countrymen*]." And so it was. On the sixtieth day the Lord
delivered me out of their hands. After a few years I was
back in Britain with my parents, who received me as their
son and begged me, after so many trials, never to leave
them again. But in a dream I saw a man from Ireland, by
name Victoricus, who carried innumerable letters, and I
read the opening portion of one which said, "The voice
of the Irish." I thought indeed to hear those beside the
Wood of Voclut, nigh to the Western Sea, and as with one
voice they cried, "Come, young man, and walk with us
again as of yore." I was so overcome that I could read no
more. Thanks be to God, who after so many years wrought
according to their cry.

II. Gaul

The Conversion of Clovis. Translated from Gregory of Tours, Historia Francorum. P.L. *71, p. 225, section xxx.*

✐   ✐   ✐

The queen never ceased to entreat the king to recognize the true God and give up idols, but nothing could move him to believe these things until he was engaged in a war with the Alemanni in which he was compelled by constraint to confess what he had refused to do voluntarily. It came to pass that his army was in danger of being wiped out. Thereupon, lifting his eyes to heaven, with compunction of heart and moved to tears, he cried, "Jesus Christ, who art according to Clotilde the Son of the living God, who art said to give aid to those in trouble and victory to those who hope in Thee. . . . I beseech Thee . . . if Thou wilt give me victory over mine enemies I will believe in Thee and be baptized in Thy name. I have called upon my gods and they are far removed from helping me. Hence I believe they are powerless, since they do not succour their followers. I now call upon Thee. Only save me from mine enemies." When he had thus spoken the Alemanni turned their backs and took to flight. . . . Clovis returning related to the queen how he had won the victory by calling upon the name of Christ. Then the queen with haste secretly summoned Remigius, the bishop of Rheims, that he should instruct the king in the word of salvation. He then began privately to tell his majesty that he should believe in the true God, the maker of heaven and earth and should give up idols. The king said, "Willingly, holy father, but there is one difficulty. My people will not give up their gods. But I will go and speak to them according to your word." But before he had opened his mouth all the people cried, "Pious king, we reject the mortal gods and are ready to follow the immortal God, whom Remigius preaches." Then the bishop with great joy gave orders to prepare the fount. The church was resplendent with banners, flickering candles and the scent of wax and incense, so that those present believed that they partook of the savor of heaven. The king asked that he be baptized by the pontiff. Like a new

Constantine Clovis ascended to the laver, putting off his former leprosy. As he went down into' the water the bishop said, "Bow thy neck. Adore what you have burned. Burn what you have adored." Now the holy bishop Remigius, a man of consummate learning and of great sanctity, may fitly be compared to the holy Sylvester [*who baptized Constantine*].

III. England

Sections from Bede's Ecclesiastical History of the English Nation, *translated by L. Gidley, (Oxford, 1870).*

A. St. Augustine before King Ethelbert. Book I, section xxv.

Having been strengthened, therefore, by the encouragement of the blessed father Gregory, Augustine, with the servants of Christ who were with him, returned to the work of the Word and came to Britain. At that time King Aedilberct [*Ethelbert*] in Kent was most powerful. . . . In this island, then, Augustine landed . . . having received, by the charge of the blessed Pope Gregory, interpreters from the nation of the Franks; and sending to Aedilberct, he gave orders to say that they had come from Rome, and brought the best message, which promised, without any doubt, to those who obeyed it, eternal joys in heaven, and a future kingdom without end with the living and true God. The king, on hearing these things, commanded them to remain in the island to which they had come, and that necessaries should be afforded them, until he should see what to do respecting them. For before this the fame of the Christian religion had reached him, inasmuch as he had a Christian wife of the royal family of the Franks, by name Bercta [*Bertha*], whom he had received from her parents upon this condition, that she might have leave to keep inviolate the rite of her faith and religion. . . . After some days, the king came to the island, and sitting in the open air, commanded Augustine with his companions to come there to conference with him. For being influenced by an ancient superstition, he had taken precaution that they should not come to him in any house, lest, on their arrival, if they had any knowledge of witchcraft, they might deceive him by taking some advantage of him. But they came endued not with demoniac but with divine virtue, bearing a silver cross for a standard, and the image of the Lord and Savior painted on a panel; and singing litanies. . . . When they preached to him the king replied, "Fair indeed are the words and the promises which you bring, but, because they are new and uncertain, I cannot give my assent to them, and leave those which for so long a time I have kept with all the nation of the Angles. . . . But we do not prohibit you from gaining by your preaching all whom ye are able to the faith of your religion." He gave them therefore an abode in the city of Doruvernis [*Canterbury*].

B. *The Synod of Whitby. Book III, section xxv.*

At this time a frequent and great question was raised concerning the keeping of the paschal feast; those who had come from Kent, as well as those who had come from Gaul, affirming that the Scots kept Easter Sunday contrary to the custom of the universal Church. . . . Queen Eanfled also, together with her court, observed it according as she had seen done in Kent . . . whence . . . it sometimes happened that the paschal feast was kept twice in one year; and when the king, having ended his fast, was keeping the Lord's paschal feast, the queen with her court still continuing in her fast, was keeping the day of Palms. [*Oswy called a synod to deal with this matter. It met at the monastery at Whitby. Colman defended the practice of the Scots and appealed to the authority of Columba. Wilfred represented the Roman practice and in concluding his defence, he asked:*] "Although your fathers were holy, is their small number, from one corner of a very remote island, to be preferred to the universal Church of Christ which is throughout the world? And even if that Columba of yours, yea, ours also, if he was Christ's, was holy . . . could be therefore he preferred to the most blessed chief of the apostles, to whom the Lord said, 'Thou art Peter, and upon this rock I will build my Church, and the gates of hell shall not prevail against it; and I will give thee the keys of the kingdom of heaven.'"?

On Wilfred's thus concluding his speech, the king said, "Is it true, Colman, that those words were said to that Peter, by the Lord?" And he said, "It is true, O king."

Then said he, "Can you show any such power given to
your Columba?" And he said, "None." And the king said
"Do you both agree on this point without any controversy,
that these words were said especially to Peter, and that the
keys of the kingdom of heaven were given him by the
Lord?" They both answered, "Yes, certainly." Then he
concluded thus, "And I tell you that he is that doorkeeper
whom I will not contradict, but as far as I know or have
any power, I desire in all things to obey his decrees, lest,
perchance, when I come to the doors of the kingdom of
heaven, there may be no one to unlock them for me, if he
is averse who is proved to have the keys."

IV. Germany

*A. The commission to Boniface by Gregory II, May 15,
719. Text in Mirbt, No. 225.*

[*After recounting the qualifications of Boniface, the
pope continues:*] Therefore in the name of the indivisible
Trinity, by the incontestible authority of the blessed Peter,
the prince of the apostles, whose doctrinal authority we
exercise by God's favor and whose sacred see we admin-
ister, we now confirm the modesty of your religion and
decree that by the word of the grace of God through
which our Lord came to send fire on the earth you should
make every effort to reach the peoples lying in the bonds
of the error of infidelity, so far as with God's help you
are able and that you show forth the service of the kingdom of God, persuading them of the truth through the
proclamation of the name of our Lord Jesus Christ and
that you instruct their untutored minds conformably with
reason through the teaching of both testaments by the
spirit of virtue, love and sobriety.

*B. The oath of Boniface to the pope. Text in Mirbt, No.
226.*

In the name of our Lord God and Savior Jesus Christ,
in the sixth year of Leo the mighty emperor crowned by
God. . . . I Boniface, bishop by the grace of God, do
solemnly promise to you blessed Peter, prince of the

apostles, and to your vicar the blessed Pope Gregory and to his successors, by the Father, Son and Holy Spirit, the inseparable Trinity, and by thy most sacred body, that I will keep the faith and purity of the holy Catholic faith and that by God's help I will persevere in the unity of the same faith, in which without doubt the salvation of Christians is comprised, and by no means will I consent to any who would seduce me from the unity of the common and universal Church but, as I said, I will in all things display my faith, purity and aid to you and to the welfare of your Church to whom our Lord God has given the power to bind and to loose and to your above named vicar and his successors. If I know of any who withstand the ancient institutions of the holy fathers I will have no communion or association with them. If I can stop them I will, and if not I will report at once to my apostolic master. And if, which God forbid, I should be induced in any way whatsoever to violate this my pledge, I shall render myself guilty before the eternal Judge and shall be subject to the penalty of Ananias and Sapphira who presumed to give you a false account of their goods. . . .

C. Charlemagne and the Saxons. Selected passages from the Capitulary. *Mirbt, No. 237.*

✔   ✔   ✔

First, with regard to all major offenses, it is our pleasure that all of the Christian churches built in Saxony be consecrated to God and held in higher honor than the shrines of the idols.

4) If any one out of despite for Christianity violates the Lenten food regulations and eats meat he shall suffer death, though the priest may judge whether he did it out of necessity.

6) If any one among the Saxons being unbaptized seeks to conceal himself and avoid baptism and to remain a pagan, he shall die the death.

11) If any one appears to his lord the king to be an infidel, he shall suffer capital punishment.

Concerning minor offenses we decree: 17) that all shall give a tenth of their labor and substance to the Church and the priests, whether noble, free born or serf, according as God has given to each.

D. Alcuin's protest against the above regulations. Letter to Charlemagne, 796 A.D., Ep. xxxiii, P.L. 100, p. 188 D.

✻   ✻   ✻

Your most holy Piety does well to consider whether it is expedient to impose the yoke of tithes on rude people who have only just embraced the faith. . . . We know that to tithe our substance is good, but better to let it pass than to lose the faith. We, indeed, who have been born, reared and taught in the Catholic faith do not readily consent to give a full tenth. How much more will a tender faith, infantile intelligence and grasping disposition be indisposed to such benevolence? . . . Of the utmost importance is it that diligence be given to preaching and the administration of baptism. But the ablution of holy baptism is of absolutely no value when applied only to the body and not preceded by a rational understanding of the Catholic faith. . . . We are not enjoined to receive the sacrament of baptism if the mind has not embraced the truth of the faith. Our Lord, in the gospels, commanded his disciples, saying, "Go, teach all nations, baptizing them. . . . [*Matt. 28:19.*] First teach, then dip.

V. Denmark

The mission of Ansgar. From Rimber, S. Anschari . . . Vita. P.L. 118, pp. 966-967. Slightly condensed.

✻   ✻   ✻

After these things it came to pass that a certain king Harald, who ruled over a part of Denmark, was expelled through the enmity of other kings. He took refuge with the most serene emperor Louis and requested his aid for the recovery of his kingdom. Louis and others urged Harald to embrace the Christian faith, pointing out how much greater would then be the intimacy between them and how much more readily Christian people [*the Franks*] would rally to his assistance if they were of the same faith. Then, with the assistance of the grace of God, Louis converted Harald, received him as he emerged from the sacred fount of baptism and adopted him as his son. When, then, by such assistance Harald regained his kingdom, he inquired whether there were not some master of the saving doctrine who could come with him and stay with him to instruct and strengthen himself and his people in the faith of the Lord. Therefore the emperor in a great assembly of nobles and priests broached the question whether there might not be some suitable volunteer. When, then, all declared that they knew of none with such devotion as to undertake so perilous a journey for the name of Christ, there arose the venerable abbot of Corbie and declared that he had just such a man among the monks of his monastery. What need to say more? Ansgar was the man and he undertook the mission.

VI. Moravia

The letter of Pope John VIII (872-82) to Swatopluk, prince of Moravia. P.L. 126, p. 905D-906D.

✓   ✓   ✓

I have inquired of your archbishop Methodious whether he accepts the symbol of the orthodox faith and whether he chants it in solemnizing the mass in accord with the faith of the Roman Church and of the six ecumenical councils. He replies that he does. We, therefore, commend him to you as your proper pastor, worthy of all reverence. And by virtue of our apostolic authority we confirm him in the archepiscopate. We order that all priests, whether Slavs or of any other race, should be obedient to him. We applaud the employment of the Slavonic tongue as reduced to writing by Constantine the philosopher [*Cyril*] in the singing of the liturgy. . . . There is nothing in faith or doctrine to impede the use of the Slavonic for the singing of the liturgy and the reading of good translations of the Old and New Testaments, or of the holy offices, for He who made the three principal languages, Hebrew, Greek and Latin, created also all others to his praise and glory. We decree, therefore, that throughout your lands, the gospel shall be read first in Latin, then in Slavonic. But you may say the mass in Latin if you prefer.

VII. Norway

King Olaf Trygveson baptizes the Country of Viken. From the Heimskringla *or the Sagas of the Norse Kings, translated by Samuel Laing (London, 1889), pp. 150-51.*

✔   ✔   ✔

When Harald Gormson, king of Denmark, had adopted
Christianity, he sent a message over all his kingdom that
all people should be baptized. . . . In Viken many were
baptized [*but subsequently lapsed*]. But now (996) that
Olaf Trygveson was king of Norway, he remained long
during the summer in Viken [*and summoning his relatives
he declared that he would*] either bring it to this that all
Norway should be Christian or die. . . . King Olaf immediately made it known to the public that he recom-
mended Christianity to all the people in his kingdom,
which message was well received and approved of by
those who had before given him their promise; and these
being the most powerful among the people assembled, the
others followed their example, and all the inhabitants of
the east part of Viken allowed themselves to be baptized.
The king then went to the north part of Viken, and invited every man to accept Christianity; and those who
opposed him he punished severely, killing some, mutilat-
ing others, and driving some into banishment. . . . During that summer (996) and the following winter (997) all
Viken was made Christian.

VIII. Russia

*The conversion of Vladimir. From the "Chronique de
Nestor," ed. Louis Leger, Publ. de l'Ecole des langues ori-
entales vivantes II, ser. XIII (Paris, 1884), condensed.*

✔   ✔   ✔

Olga went to Constantinople. The emperor then was
Constantine VII. Observing that she was exceeding fair
and wise he said, "You are worthy to reign with us in this
city." She answered, "I am a pagan. If you want to baptize
me, do it yourself. Otherwise I will not be baptized." Then
the emperor baptized her with the assistance of the patriarch. Once enlightened she rejoiced in body and soul and
the patriarch said to her, "Blessed art thou among the
women of Russia, for thou hast loved the light and rejected the darkness. The sons of Russia will bless thee
until the last generation." As a sponge which takes up
water she received his instructions. Then the emperor
wanted to marry her, but she said, "What! You want to

marry me? Yet you baptized me and called me your daughter. This is against the law of the Christians and you know it very well." The emperòr said, "Olga, you have tricked me." He gave her presents and she returned to Kiev where she lived with her son Sviatoslav. She tried to convert him but he said, "Take up a foreign faith! My droujina [*retainers*] will laugh at me." Olga said, "If you do it, they will all do it too." But he persisted in paganism. He was killed in battle and his skull made into a drinking cup. He reigned twenty-eight years. (d. 972) His son Vladimir, having displaced his brother, began to reign in 978. Now in the year 986 some Bulgarians came to him and said, "You are a wise prince, but you have no religion. Accept Mohammed." Vladimir said, "What is your faith?" They answered, "We believe in God. Mohammed taught us to be circumcized, not to eat pork or drink wine and promised that in heaven we might enjoy ourselves with many women." Vladimir was pleased as to the women but repelled by circumcision and abstinence from pork and wine. Then came the Roman Catholics and said, "We have been sent by the pope." "And what are your commandments?" asked Vladimir. "Fast as much as you can. Eat and drink always to the glory of God." Vladimir said, "Our ancestors would have none of that." Then came the Jews who complained that the Christians worshipped one whom they had crucified. Their rule was circumcision, abstinence from pork and rabbit and observance of the Sabbath. "Where is your country?" asked Vladimir. "Jerusalem." "Do you live there now?" "No. God was displeased with our fathers and gave our country to the Christians." "Very well," said Vladimir, "if God has rejected you, why do you teach others?" Then came a Greek who reproached the Romans with using a wafer instead of bread in the sacrament of the altar. He then gave a long exposition of the faith, ending with an account of the judgment day and the woes pronounced on those rejected. Vladimir groaned and sent delegations to observe the practice of these religions in their own lands. The report was that the liturgy of the Greeks was ravishing. No spectacle on earth could approach it. There God dwells with men. The bogars then assured Vladimir that if the religion of the Greeks were bad Olga would not have received it. And he said, "Where then shall we be baptized?"

— Reading No. 3 —

THE CHURCH AND
THE CIVIL RULERS

I. Gelasius I (492-496 A.D.) instructs the Emperor Anastasius of the limits of his power. Ed. XII, 494 A.D. Mirbt, No. 187.

✓   ✓   ✓

There are indeed two [*powers*], most august Emperor, by which chiefly this world is ruled, the sacred authority of the pontiffs and the royal power. Of the two the priesthood has the greater weight to the degree that it must render an account for kings themselves in matters divine. Know then, most clement son, that although you preside with dignity in human affairs, as to the divine you are to submit your neck to those from whom you look for salvation and from whom you receive the celestial sacraments. You are to be subject rather than to rule in the religious sphere and bow to the judgment of the priests rather than seek to bend them to your will. For, if in the area of public discipline the priests recognize your authority as derived from above and obey your laws, lest in purely secular matters they should appear to resist, how much more willingly should you obey them who are charged with the administration of the venerable mysteries? . . . And if it is proper that the hearts of the faithful should be submitted to priests in general, by how much more should obedience be rendered to him who presides over that see which the Highest Divinity desired to be preeminent above all priests [*i.e., the see of Rome*]?

II. Gregory II's defiance of Leo III. 715-731 A.D. From the Greek published by Erich Caspar, "Papst Gregor II und der Bilderstreit," Zeitsschrift für Kirchengeschichte 52 *(1933). Greatly condensed.*

✓ ✓ ✓

August Emperor, you are quite right that Moses forbad the making of images, but that was because they were of false gods, but when God introduced a new dispensation in the incarnation of His Son, the saints and martyrs were then portrayed as in life and it was entirely proper to reverence their images rather than those of the devil. Likewise Christ at the request of King Abgar sent him his picture. Why then, you ask, do we not portray God the Father? Because we do not know what He looks like. As a brother in Christ we beseech you to return to the truth which you have forsaken. The love of Christ knows that when we come into the church of the blessed Peter and look upon the likeness of the saint our tears fall like a freshet from the clouds. Christ caused the blind to see. You make them blind. You claim that we worship rocks, walls and planks. Not at all, O king! It is for remembrance and to lift our thick and torpid minds on high. We do not worship the images as gods. What a ghastly thought! Nor do we place our hope in them. But if there is an image of our Lord, we say, "Lord Jesus Christ help us and save us." If the image be of His holy Mother we say, "Holy Mother of God, Mother of the Lord, pray to Thy Son for the salvation of our souls." And if it be of a martyr we say, "Holy Stephen, proto-martyr, who didst shed thy blood for Christ, as having boldness, pray for us." Turn from your wicked ways, O king. You say, "Hezekiah, king of the Jews, after eight hundred years removed the brazen serpent from the temple and I after eight hundred years have removed the images." You are indeed a brother of the tyrant, Hezekiah, who removed the sign sanctified by God, that as through the serpent came the damnation of Adam and Eve, so through the brazen serpent came the healing of the people. When we come into the church and see the Holy Mother giving milk to the babe in her arms with angels around singing, Holy, Holy, Holy, we come out stupefied. Who would not be wounded in heart and weep? When we enter the baptistry and see the priests standing in a circle, when we behold the Supper of the Lord, the giving of sight to the blind, the raising of

Lazarus, the healing of the leper and the paralytic, the miracle of the loaves and the baskets of the fragments, the transfiguration, the crucifixion, the resurrection, the ascension and the coming of the Spirit—who can behold Abraham with knife uplifted against the throat of Isaac, who at these sights is not smitten with tears?

You propose to call an ecumenical synod. Know, O king, that dogmas are the affair of the holy Church, not of kings but of priests. The congruence of kings devoted to Christ and of blessed high priests when all is done in peace and love is a single power, but you have plunged a sword into the peace of the Church. Stop and be silent. You threaten to sent to Rome and knock down the statue of St. Peter and bind Gregory the pontiff as Constantine did to Martin. Bear in mind that the pontiffs who in peace preside in Rome are the dividing wall between East and West and if you bluster and threaten us we have no need to argue with you. The Roman pontiff has only to go three miles into the Campania. Then, cheery-o, you can chase the wind. We beseech you to give up your foolish and childish ways. You know that your empire does not extend to Rome, save for the city because of the proximity of the sea and your fleet, but, as we said, the pope need only go three miles to be beyond your range. It is a crying shame that whereas rustics and barbarians have become civilized, a civilized person like you has become a barbarian. The whole of the West lays its trophies before the holy prince of the apostles and if you send troops to destroy the image of St. Peter, beware. We warn you ahead of time. We are innocent of the blood that will be shed. It will recoil on your neck and head.

III. The Condemnation of Images in Constantinople, 754 A.D. Post Nicene Fathers, *series second, vol. 14, pp. 543-544.*

Under the guidance of the Holy Spirit, we found that the unlawful art of painting living creatures blasphemed the fundamental doctrine of our salvation—namely, the Incarnation of Christ. What avails the folly of the painter who with his polluted hands tries to fashion that which should only be believed in the heart and confessed with the mouth? He makes an image and calls it Christ. The name Christ signifies *God and man*. Consequently he has depicted the Godhead which cannot be represented. They take refuge in the excuse, "We represent only the flesh of Christ." But how do the fools venture to separate the flesh from the Godhead? They fall into the abyss of impiety because they ascribe to the flesh a subsistence of its own and thus introduce a fourth person into the Trinity. . . . But if some say, we may be right in regard to the images of Christ, but it is not right for us to forbid also the images of the altogether spotless and ever-glorious Mother of God, we reply that Christianity has rejected the whole of heathenism. If any one thinks to call the saints back again to life by a dead art, discovered by the heathen, he makes himself guilty of blasphemy. Who dares with heathenish art to paint the Mother of God? Scripture says, "God is a spirit," and again, "Thou shalt not make thee any graven image."

IV. The Donation of Constantine. 757-767 A.D. Mirbt, No. 228, condensed.

✔   ✔   ✔

In the name of the sacred and undivided Trinity, we the Emperor Constantine send greetings to the blessed father of fathers, Sylvester, bishop and pope of Rome, and to all his successors who sit in the seat of the blessed Peter to the end of time. We wish it to be known that we have renounced the cult of idols in accord with the teaching of our pontiff Sylvester and have embraced the faith of the perfect Trinity. Our Lord God Himself had compassion on me, a sinner, and by the light of His Splendor illumined my darkness. In the flesh I was a leper and the doctors at Rome advised that I bathe in the blood of infants, who thereupon were assembled to be slaughtered. But when our Serenity heard the wails of the mothers I had compassion on them and they were returned in public conveyances. That same night the apostles Peter and Paul appeared to me in a dream and told me that because of this act of mercy, Christ would cure me. I should seek out Sylvester, bishop of Rome, who because of persecution was hiding in a cave. I repaired to him and asked who were these gods, Peter and Paul. "Not gods," said he, "but apostles of our Savior, the Lord Jesus Christ." He showed me their images and I recognized at once the likeness. Then the blessed father Sylvester enjoined penances and having baptized me three times I was cured of my leprosy. I perceived that there is no other god than the Father, Son and Spirit. Sylvester explained what authority had been conferred upon the blessed Peter when the Lord said, "Thou art Peter, etc.," and again, "To thee I will give the keys of the kingdom of heaven, etc." Then I decreed that the blessed Roman church should have greater honor than the empire and preeminence over the churches of Antioch, Alexandria, Constantinople and Jerusalem. We transferred to these blessed apostles, to the blessed Sylvester and his successors, our Lateran palace together with the diadem, crown, scepter and imperial vestments. Likewise to the power and jurisdiction of the blessed pontiff we commit the city of Rome as well as Italy and the western provinces. And we remove our empire and kingly power to Byzantium, because where the head of the Christian religion, instituted by the divine Emperor, is situated, there it is not fitting that the earthly emperor should exercise sway.

V. The coronation of Charlemagne

A. From Einhard, Vita Caroli Magni. *Mirbt, No. 240.*

✓   ✓   ✓

Because of the maltreatment of Pope Leo III and at his request Charles came to Rome and spent the whole winter composing the affairs of the Church, at which time he received the title of emperor and augustus. To this at first he was averse and affirmed that had he known what the pope was going to do he would not have entered the church that day even if it was an especially holy day. But his great patience mollified the umbrage of the Roman emperors [*at Constantinople*] at his assumption of the title.

B. From the Annales Laureshamenses. *Mirbt, No. 242.*

✓   ✓   ✓

Because the title of emperor had lapsed among the Greeks, inasmuch as a woman exercised the office, therefore it seemed to the apostolic Leo and to all the holy fathers in council and to the remaining Christian people that Charles, the king of the Franks, should bear the title of emperor because he held the city of Rome itself where the Caesars had always resided as well as Italy, Gaul and Germany. Seeing that the omnipotent God had given these territories into his power, it appeared to them just that with the aid of God and the consent of the universal Church he should have the name itself. Charles was not able to deny their petition and subjecting himself in all humility to God and to the entreaty of the clergy and of the universal Christian people, on the day of the nativity of the Lord Jesus Christ, he received the name of emperor with consecration by Pope Leo.

C. Liber Pontificalis. *Mirbt, No. 248.*

On the day of the nativity of our Lord Jesus Christ in the said basilica of the blessed Peter the apostle, all were again gathered. Then the venerable and beneficent pontiff with his own hands crowned Charles with a crown. Thereupon all of the faithful Romans, seeing such love and defense as he had rendered to the holy Roman church and its vicar, cried out with one voice at the instance of the blessed Peter, the key bearer of the kingdom of heaven, "To Charles, the most pious augustus, crowned of God, to the great peace-loving emperor, life and victory." Three times they cried and by all he was constituted *imperator Romanorum.* Thereupon the most holy primate and pontiff anointed with oil the holy Charles, the most excellent son, the king, on the very day of the nativity of our Lord Jesus Christ.

VI. Dionysius the Areopagite, The Celestial and the Ecclesiastical Hierarchies. *Text and French translation of the first: "Denys L'Aréopagite 'Hierarchie Celeste,' " ed. René Roques,* Sources Chrétiennes *(Paris, 1958). Cf.* Oeuvres completes du Pseudo-Denys l'Aréopagite, *tr. Maurice de Gandillac (Paris, 1943). From* The Celestial Hierarchy, *III, 1 and 2.*

The hierarchy in my view is a sacred order and intelligence and energy assimilating itself, in so far as it may, to the form divine, ascending by analogy to the divine by virtue of the illuminations accorded thence. The beauty then which beseems God, being simple, good, initial and final, unalloyed and wholely devoid of the dissimilar, confers upon each according to merit something of the light supernal and perfects the devotees in divine imitation by conforming them harmoniously to its own immutable form. The object of the hierarchy, then, is, in so far as may be possible, an assimilation and union with God, whom she accepts as the master of all holy intelligences and energy. On Him her gaze is fixed without wavering. From Him she receives, as best she may, the mark of His imprint. Then she makes her initiation into images of the divine, mirrors without blemish, reflecting to perfection, able to receive the primordial light of the thearchic ray, inundated with holy radiance. The initiates in turn become the illuminators of those who come after them according to the thearchic order. When, then, one speaks of the hierarchy, one has in mind a certain sacred disposition, an image of the thearchic splendor, which through the hierarchic intelligence accomplishes the mysteries of its own illumination and assimilates them, in so far as possible, to its own being.

VII. The Coronation of Edgar, described by a monk of the cloister, 995-1005 A.D. Edited by Percy Ernst Schramm, "Die Krönung bei den Westfranken und Angelsachsen von 878 um 1000." Zeitschrift der Savigny stiftung f. Rechsgeschichte *54, Kan. Abt. 23 (1955), pp. 231-233.*

✦   ✦   ✦

According to custom the archbishops and all the other distinguished priests, abbots and abbesses and all the dukes and prefects and judges assembled, from the east and from the west, from the north and from the sea as an edict went forth from the emperor that they should gather unto him. This glorious and admirable army of his people came not that they might deliver him unto death and hang him upon a tree as the lamentable Jews did to the gentle Jesus, but with rational intelligence and joy they gathered and the most reverend bishops blessed, anointed and consecrated, the bestowal coming from Christ, by whom and from whom the blessed unction of the highest benediction and holy religion proceeds. Then were manifest the glorious festivity and the solemnity of the Holy Spirit when all came to consecrate the glorious king whose scepter was refulgent with glory and whose diadem resplendent with the beauty of gold. A glorious procession led the king to the church. Two bishops received him and laying aside his diadem he prostrated himself before the altar. Then Dunstan, the chief of the bishops, chanted the *Te Deum*. The king was raised up and made his promise to protect the church and maintain justice. The archbishop recited prayers as likewise did Oswald [*of York*]. After the consecration they anointed him and sang the antiphon, "Zadok anointed Solomon." After the anointing the archbishop gave him a ring, girt him with a sword and placed a crown upon his head. He was given also a scepter and a rod. The most distinguished bishops, the venerable Dunstan and the reverend Oswald, were then elevated together with the king. All the excellence of the Angles shone forth gloriously rejoicing in the supernal King who had deigned to give them a king. The queen arrayed in fine linen with emeralds and pearls, together with the abbots and abbesses, provided a banquet, after which all withdrew wishing their majesties the tranquility of peace.

— Reading No. 4 —

THE UPSURGE OF THE CHURCH

I. The Charter of Cluny given by Duke William of Aquitaine, Sept., 11, 910. Alexander Bruel, Recueil des Chartres de L'Abbaye de Cluny *1 (Paris, 1876), Doc. 112.*

✓   ✓   ✓

Plainly God has supplied rich men with an avenue to eternal reward if they rightly employ their transitory possessions. Wherefore, I William, by the grace of God duke

and count, earnestly considering how I may further my
salvation, while yet there is time, have deemed it expedient, in fact eminently necessary, that I should devote some
of my temporal goods to the profit of my soul. No better
way to this end appears than that, in the words of the
Lord, I should make the poor my friends (Lk. 16:9), and
should support a company of monks out of my substance
in perpetuity. Be it known, then, to all who live in the
unity of the faith of Christ, that for the love of our Lord
and Savior Jesus Christ I transfer from my lordship to the
holy apostles Peter and Paul the town of Cluny together
with the manor demesne, the chapel in honor of Mary the
blessed Mother of God and St. Peter, the prince of the
apostles, together with all that pertains thereunto: villas,
chapels, serfs male and female, vines, fields, meadows,
woods, waters and their outlets, mills, incomes and revenues, lands tilled and untilled in their entirety. I William
and my wife Ingelborga give all these to the said apostles,
first for the love of God and then for the soul of my lord
Odo the king, of my father and mother, for me and my
wife, for our bodies and souls. A regular monastery shall
be constructed at Cluny, the monks to follow the rule of
St. Benedict. They shall there ardently pursue celestial
converse and sedulously offer prayers and petitions to the
Lord, both for me and for all. The monks and their possessions are to be under the abbot Berno and thereafter of
one of their number elected in accord with the pleasure
of God and the rule of St. Benedict. Neither by our power
nor any other shall they be deterred from making a canonical election. Every five years they are to pay to the
church of the apostles at Rome five solidi for lights. We
desire that they should daily exercise works of mercy to
the poor, indigent, strangers and pilgrims. The monks
shall not be subject to us, our parents, the royal power
or any other terrestrial authority. By God and in God and
all the saints and the terrible day of judgment I objure
and warn that no secular prince, or count whatsoever, or
the pontiff of the see of Rome shall invade the possessions
of the servants of God, alienate, diminish, exchange, give
away as a benefice, or set any prelate over them without
their consent. If any man does this, let his name be erased
from the book of life. He will have against him the chief
key bearer of the celestial monarchy together with St.

Paul and in accord with the law on earth he shall be fined a hundred pounds of gold.

Signed by William and Ingelborga [*and a number of others whose names are written in the* Lamb's Book of Life, *but are otherwise forgotten*]

II. The Truce of God and the Peace of God

A. The spread of the movement. Raoul Glaber, Les Cinq Livres de ses Histoires *900-1044, ed. Maurice Prou,* Collections des Textes *I (Paris, 1886), pp. 103-104.*

✓　　　✓　　　✓

In the thousandth year from the passion of the Lord [*1033*] the face of heaven smiled with placid serenity, exhibiting the magnanimity of the Creator and great abundance succeeded to the previous scarcity. At that time, therefore, the bishops and the abbots, first in Aquitaine, summoned synods of all the people to which many relics of the saints were brought. Thereupon the provinces of Arles, Lyons, the whole of Burgundy and the remoter parts of France decreed that councils should convene for the fostering of peace and faith. A great multitude hearing this, from the greatest to the very least, were prepared to obey whatever the pastors of the churches might decree no less than if a voice had spoken to men from heaven. The most important decision had to do with conserving the peace inviolable so that men of any condition at enmity with the king might without fear lay down their arms. No one should prey upon or invade the territory of another and if he did should be punished by fine or severe corporal penalty. The sacred precincts of all churches should be so respected that any criminal there seeking asylum should be immune, save one who had broken the peace. Clerics, monks and pilgrims should be unmolested in travelling.

B. The Oath of Robert the Pious. Charles Pfister, Etudes sur le Règne de Robert le Pieux *996-1031 (Paris, 1885) Doc. xii, pp. lx-lxi.*

✓　　　✓　　　✓

The oath submitted by Warren, the archbishop of Beauvais to Robert the Pious, and sworn to by him: I will not infringe in any way upon the Church. I will not attack a cleric or monk if unarmed, nor will I take their horse unless they are at fault, or after fifteen days have not heeded my remonstrance. I will not take as booty an ox, cow, pig, wether, lamb, goat, ass and its load, nor a mare with a colt. I will not attack a vilain or a vilainess or servants, or merchants, nor steal their money, nor hold them for ransom. I will not take from any man a mule, male or female, or a stallion, a mare or a colt in pasture from the calends of March to the feast of All Saints, except to recover a debt. I will not burn houses unless I find an enemy knight or robber inside. I will not cut down or root out the vines of another. I will not assail nor rob unless it is their fault. I will not attack noble ladies travelling without their husbands unless it is their fault, nor widows and nuns. From the beginning of Lent to the end of Easter I will not attack an unarmed knight, nor rob him of his goods.

III. The First Crusade

A. The speech of Urban II at the Council of Clermont, 1095. Conflated from several versions translated in Dana Carlton Munro, "Urban and the Crusaders," Translations and Reprints (University of Pennsylvania, 1901).

✓   ✓   ✓

O race of the Franks, we learn that in some of your provinces no one can venture on the road by day or by night without injury or attack by highwaymen, and no one is secure even at home. Let us then re-enact the law of our ancestors known as the Truce of God. And now that you have promised to maintain the peace among yourselves you are obligated to succour your brethren in the East, menaced by an accursed race, utterly alienated from God. The Holy Sepulchre of our Lord is polluted by the filthiness of an unclean nation. Recall the greatness of Charlemagne. O most valiant soldiers, descendants of invincible ancestors, be not degenerate. Let all hatred depart from among you, all quarrels end, all wars cease. Start upon the road to the Holy Sepulchre to wrest that land from the wicked race and subject it to yourselves.

B. The Capture of Jerusalem in 1099. Raymond of Agiles, Historia Francorum, *tr. Frederick Duncalf and*

August C. Krey, Parallel Source Problems in Medieval History (*New York, Harper & Bros., 1912*).

✓ ✓ ✓

Some of our men (and this was more merciful) cut off the heads of their enemies; others shot them with arrows, so that they fell from the towers; others tortured them longer by casting them into the flames. Piles of heads, hands, and feet were to be seen in the streets of the city. It was necessary to pick one's way over the bodies of men and horses. But these were small matters compared to what happened at the temple of Solomon, a place where religious services are ordinarily chanted. What happened there? If I tell the truth, it will exceed your powers of belief. So let it suffice to say this much at least, that in the temple and portico of Solomon, men rode in blood up to their knees and the bridle reins. Indeed, it was a just and splendid judgment of God, that this place should be filled with the blood of the unbelievers, when it had suffered so long from their blasphemies.

Now that the city was taken it was worth all our previous labors and hardships to see the devotion of the pilgrims at the Holy Sepulchre. How they rejoiced and exulted and sang the ninth chant to the Lord. It was the ninth day, the ninth joy and exaltation, and of perpetual happiness. The ninth sermon, the ninth chant was demanded by all. This day, I say, will be famous in all future ages, for it turned our labors and sorrows into joy and exultation; this day, I say, marks the justification of all Christianity and the humiliation of paganism; our faith was renewed. "The Lord made this day, and we rejoiced and exulted in it," (Ps. 118:24) for on this day the Lord revealed Himself to His people and blessed them.

C. Deus non vult. *Ralph Niger,* De Re Militare, *published from manuscript by George B. Flahiff,* "Deus non vult: *a critic of the third crusade."* Medieval Studies *IX* (*1947*), *pp. 162-188.*

✓ ✓ ✓

The Saracens have recently reconquered the promised land. The king and his nobles are captive. The temple, the Holy Sepulchre and the wood of the Holy Cross are in polluted hands. Because of our sins Palestine is given over to our enemies. The wrath of the Lord has descended upon Christians because they were unwilling to be one finger behind Saladin in riches. But what has happened there is less of a menace than the heresies of the Manichees and many other interdicted sects which swarm in these times. Illiterates desert the churches and the clergy. They deny the sacraments of the Church, say that the eucharist is mere bread, reject infant baptism and the sacrament of marriage and affirm many other blasphemies with such boldness that they are ready to die for their assertion. Rather than accept penance they are ready to be penalized by death and walk into the flames as if they were dew. By good deeds they spread nefarious opinions. When, then, such despite is done to the faith at home what hope is there that the occident can help the orient? What good will it be if Palestine is delivered from the Saracens if infidelity flourishes at home?

Besides, are the Saracens to be killed because God has given them Palestine? Does not God say, "I desire not the death of the sinner"? (Ezek. 33:11.) The Saracens are men of like nature with ourselves. They may be repelled if they invade our territory, because force may be repelled by force, but the medicine is not to exceed the disease. They are to be smitten with the sword of the spirit that they may come voluntarily to the faith, because God hates forced service. The Lord Pope, the vicar of God on earth has offered indulgences for the remission of all sins to those who go on pilgrimages. I will not contest his competence, but God does not remit penalties until after sins have been repudiated. And what shall we say of the participation of so many clerics who are not permitted to pollute their sacred hands by bloodshed?

IV. The Gregorian Reform

A. Clerical celibacy. Libelli de Lite, MGH II (1892). Bernaldi Presbyteri Adversus quondam Alboinum Presbiterum.

✓   ✓   ✓

If the laity according to the Apostle Paul should abstain from their wives during a period of prayer (I Cor. 7:5), how much more should the priests never again from the day of their ordination cohabit with their wives, seeing that priests are dedicated to the daily office of prayer and the administration of baptism and the sacrifice of the Mass?

B. The Mass not to be received from concubinous priests. Ibid. *III (1897). Epistola de vitanda missa uxoratorum sacerdotum, p. 2.*

✓   ✓   ✓

I can hardly open my eyes for rage against the wolfish heretics and the assinine Catholics who, after the admonitions of innumerable councils and the anathemas of Roman pontiffs and the condemnation of all the Catholic bishops, now, as if nothing had happened, would refer to the judgment of bishops who consist of their own heresiarchs, the question whether we should completely avoid the priests condemned for fornication, whereas Paul says that with such we should not so much as eat (I Cor. 5:11). He who communicates with the excommunicated is himself excommunicated, and the simoniacs and the Nicolaitans were excommunicated in the great synod of Gregory VII in 1078.

C. Whether the pope may introduce an innovation. Ibid. *I (1891). Petri Damiani Disceptatio Synodalis, pp. 80-81. A dialogue between advocates of king and church.*

✓   ✓   ✓

King's advocate: You cannot deny that the father of my lord the king, the Emperor Henry of pious memory, received [*at the Roman synod of 1045*] the perpetual right of electing the pope, which right was confirmed to my lord the king by Pope Nicholas II [*at the synod of Sutri in 1059*]. If a private individual should not give up his right until the matter has been judicially determined, should then the royal majesty give up this prerogative of his dignity, which he received through the liberality of the apostolic see and which he inherited by the right of imperial eminence from his father? In what way does one, who has not offended the Roman Church, lose without due process his right of dignity in the Roman Church?
The Church's advocate: The Roman Church is much more

sublime than the king's mother according to the flesh. Although the king is an excellent youth everyone knows he is a boy. And who does not know that a boy is not competent to choose a priest? During his minority his mother disposes of everything. If, then, the mother after the flesh may help her son in matters terrestrial, shall not Mother Church aid her son, the king, in matters spiritual? Frequently a change of circumstance requires that things be done differently. Recall that when the Roman church elected a pope [*1061*] there was such rioting that it was not possible to wait for a decision from the royal clemency at so great a remove. It was necessary as quickly as possible to choose a head, lest the citizens inflict on each other mutual wounds and many be slain.

King's advocate: Say what you please, argue as you like, what the pope commands, what a council confirms and what a written document affirms ought by no means to be changed.

Church's advocate: Why should not the statutes of frail humanity be changed when the Omnipotent God, who knows the future, changes what He has established?

King's advocate: When did God ever do that?

Church's advocate: When Noah was five hundred years old God told him He would grant the world only one hundred and twenty more years of grace, and then when Noah was six hundred years old He let loose the flood. Thus we see that God changed His mind about the extra twenty years. (Gen. 5:32; 6:3; 7:11).

D. The Dictatus Papae *of Gregory VII. Mirbt, No. 278.*

[*Passages affecting the Church*]: The Roman church was founded by the Lord alone and only the Roman pontiff may rightfully be called universal. He alone may depose or reinstate bishops. His legate takes precedence over all others in a council. He may transfer bishops from see to see. By no one may he be judged and no one shall condemn an appellant to the Holy See. The Roman church has never erred and, according to the testimnoy of Scripture, never will in perpetuity. He cannot be considered a Catholic who is not in accord with the Roman church.

[*Passages affecting the state*]: The feet of the pope alone are to be kissed by all princes. The pope may depose emperors and absolve subjects from fealty to iniquitous rulers.

V. The Investiture Controversy

The documents in this section and a number besides are fully translated by Ernest F. Henderson in Select Historical Documents of the Middle Ages (*London, 1910*) *from the text of M. Doeberl,* Mon. Germ. Selecta *111* (*München, 1889*), *p. 16 ff. Those by Gregory VII himself are fully translated by Ephraim Emerton in "The Correspondence of Gregory VII,"* Records of Civilization *XIV* (*New York, 1932*) *from the text of Erich Caspar,* Register Gregors VII, *2 vols.* (*1920, 1923*). *The selections here presented are condensed and freshly translated.*

A. Prohibition of Investitures, Nov. 19, 1078.

Since we have learned that in many places investiture of churches is being made by lay persons contrary to the statutes of the holy fathers and that in consequence many disturbances have arisen in the Church by which the Christian religion comes into despite, we decree that no cleric shall receive investiture of a bishopric, abbacy or a church from the hands of an emperor, king or any other lay person, man or woman. If he presumes to do so, let him know that the investiture is devoid of apostolic authority and that he shall remain excommunicated pending condign satisfaction.

B. The letter of Gregory VII to Henry IV, Dec. 8, 1075.

It seems to us very strange that you should profess yourself in all humility to be a devoted son of Mother Church with reverential sweetness and then in fact should show yourself to be an acrid enemy of those canonical and apostolic decrees which the religion of the Church deems most essential. Not to mention other matters, take the case of Milan. Your conduct shows how little you keep the pledges you made through your mother and through the bishops we sent to you. And now, adding wound to wound, you have given the churches of Fermo and Spoleto to certain persons not even known to us.

In this very year a synod was held, over which we presided by divine dispensation. Here it was observed that the Christian religion has recently been deteriorating and through the strategems of Satan the means for gaining souls are trodden under foot. Moved by the manifest peril of the ruin of the Lord's flock, we determined to return to the decrees and doctrine of the holy fathers. We have decreed nothing new, no invention of our own, but only that error should be abandoned and we should go back to the one and only rule of ecclesiastical discipline and the well trodden path of the saints.

C. *The Reply of Henry IV to Gregory VII, Jan. 24, 1076.*

Henry, king not by usurpation, but by the holy ordinance of God to Hildebrand, not now pope but a false monk: this greeting you deserve because there is no order in the Church which you have not brought into confusion and dishonor. To mention just a few especial cases, you have not only not feared to touch the rulers of the Church, anointed by Christ, archbishops, bishops and priests, but you have trodden on them like serfs. We have put up with this out of regard for your Apostolic See, but you have taken our humility for fear and have not hesitated to lift a hand against the royal power conferred on us by God and have threatened to deprive us of it, as if we had received the kingship from you, as if kingship and empire were not in the hands of God. Our Lord Jesus Christ called us to the kingship, but did not call you to the priesthood. The steps in your ascent were these: by guile you obtained money, by money favor, by favor the sword and with the sword you have mounted the throne of peace and from the throne of peace you have cast out peace, arming subjects against their prelates, giving the laity power to depose or contemn priests. And you have ventured to touch me, anointed no matter how unworthily to the kingship, subject according to the tradition of the holy fathers only to God and not to be deposed save for defection from the faith, which God forbid, St. Peter said, "Fear God, honor the king," and Paul pronounced on one who should preach another gospel the curse of anathema. To this curse by the judgment of all our bishops you are subject. Come down, then, from the usurped apostolic seat. Let another ascend who will preach the sound doctrine of the blessed apostle without the cloak of violence. I Henry, king by the grace of God, and all my bishops say, "Come down, come down and be forever damned."

D. Letter of the German bishops to Gregory VII, Jan. 24, 1076. Their names and sees are listed at the start.

✓   ✓   ✓

The German bishops to Brother Hildebrand: When you first invaded the government of the Church, although we knew perfectly well how illicit and nefarious was your arrogance in presuming to go counter to established procedure, nevertheless we dissimulated in charitable silence, hoping that your criminal beginning would be rectified, but now the lamentable state of the universal Church proclaims and deplores that to bad beginnings have been added worse, for whereas our Lord and Savior impressed upon the faithful the singular good of charity and peace, you, as the standard bearer of schism, lacerate all the members of the Church hitherto living in tranquillity, and the flame of discord, which you kindled among the dire factions at Rome, now with furious dementia you disseminate throughout the churches of Italy, Germany, Gaul and Spain. You have done your best to take away from bishops all of the power which was conferred upon them from God through the Holy Spirit. You have turned over all ecclesiastical administration to the fury of the mob, since no one can exercise the office of priest or bishop unless he has cravenly supplicated your Munificence. By your glorious decrees, which cannot be mentioned without tears, the name of Christ has well nigh perished. Who would not gasp at the indignity that you should arrogate to yourself a new and unlawful power to destroy the due rights of the entire fraternity? You go so far as to say that none of us, but only you, has the right to bind and loose if a crime by one of our parishoners is taken to you or merely comes to your notice. We cannot complain enough of the outrages you have done to bishops whom you call the sons of harlots. Therefore, since your accession was

initiated by such perjuries and since the Church of God
sinks to ruin by reason of the terrific storm occasioned
through your innovations and since your life is besmirched
by ill report, we renounce the obedience we never promised you and will not observe it for the future, but as you
say we are not bishops, so we say you are not pope.

*E. The First Deposition of Henry IV by Gregory VII,
Feb. 22, 1076.*

✦   ✦   ✦

Blessed Peter, Prince of the apostles, incline I beseech
thee, thy pious ears to us and hear thy servant, whom
thou hast reared from infancy and protected until this
day from mine enemies. Thou art my witness, thou and
my Lady the Mother of God and the blessed Paul, thy
brother among all the saints, that I did not willingly assume the governance of the holy Roman Church. I did
not ascend to thy see by rapine. Rather I desired to finish my life in pilgrimage than to seize thy place for the
glory of the world. Therefore I believe that it is of thy
grace and not of my works that it hath and doth please
thee that the Christian people especially committed to
thee should be obedient to me. The power to act in thy
stead was particularly committed to me by God, to bind
and to loose in heaven and on earth. In this confidence,
then, for the honor and defense of thy Church, on behalf
of God the omnipotent, Father, Son and Holy Ghost, by
thy power and authority I deprive Henry the King, son
of Henry the Emperor, who has risen against thy Church
with unparalleled pride, of the governance of all Germany
and Italy and I absolve all Christians from the bond of
the oath which they have or shall make. I prohibit any
one from serving him as king. . . . In thy stead I bind
him in the bonds of anathema, that all nations may know
that thou art Peter and on this rock I will build my
Church, and the gates of hell shall not prevail against it.

*F. Gregory VII to Bishop Hermann of Metz, March 15,
1081.*

✦   ✦   ✦

Shall not a dignity [*the empire*] instituted by layman,
even those ignorant of God, be subject to that dignity

which the providence of almighty God instituted for His honor and granted it out of mercy to the world? whose Son, indubitably both God and man, high priest above all priests, sitting at the right hand of God the Father, rendering for us perpetual intercession, despised the kingdom of the world, by which the sons of the world are inflated, and of his own will went to the priesthood of the cross. Who will deny that kings and princes have their beginning from those who ignorant of God seek by pride, rapine, perfidy, homicide and almost every crime, at the instigation of the devil, the prince of this world, to dominate over their fellows in blind arrogance and intolerable presumption? . . . Many pontiffs have excommunicated sometimes kings, sometimes emperors. . . . Pope Zachary deposed the King of the Franks, not so much for crime as for incompetence and replaced him by Pippin, the father of Charlemagne. . . . Every king, when he comes to die, must beseech the aid of a priest to save him from hell, but what priest or even layman turned to a king for his salvation? Let not the rulers try to make the Church a handmaid, for if we should honor earthly parents how much more the spiritual?

— Reading No. 5 —

THE RENAISSANCE OF THE TWELFTH CENTURY

1. The Beginnings of Scholasticism

A. Anselm's search for a single proof of God's existence. Eadmeri Historia Novorum in Anglia et opuscula duo de Vita Sancti Anselmi, *ed. Martin Rule (Rolls Series, 1884), p. 333.*

✦   ✦   ✦

The thought came into the mind of Anselm to see whether he could prove by one brief argument that which is believed and preached about God, namely that He is eternal, intelligible, omnipotent, everywhere whole, incomprehensible, just, pious, merciful, faithful, truth, goodness, justice and whatever more and how all of these are one in Him. This effort gave him the greatest difficulty. Pondering on the question disturbed not only his appetite for food and drink, as well as his sleep, but what was much worse, his devotions. Observing this he decided that the very attempt was a temptation of the devil and he tried to put it from him. The more he sweated the more this cogitation plagued him, and behold on a certain night, between the nocturnal vigils, the grace of God shone in his heart, the matter appeared clear to his mind and his whole being was filled with immense delight and jubilation.

B. Anselm's ontological argument. Monologium, P.L. *158, pp. 223-227.*

✔   ✔   ✔

I sought if I might find a single argument which would alone suffice to demonstrate that God exists. This I did in the spirit of faith seeking understanding. . . . Come now, O Lord my God, teach my heart where and how it may seek Thee. O Lord, if Thou art not here where shall I seek Thee absent, and if Thou art everywhere why do I not see Thee present? Surely Thou dwellest in light inaccessible. When wilt Thou enlighten our eyes? I do not presume to penetrate Thy profundity but only in some measure to understand Thy truth, which my heart believes and loves, for I seek not to understand that I may believe, but I believe in order that I may understand.

Now the fool will admit that there can be in the mind something than which nothing greater can be conceived. This, being understood, is in the mind, but it cannot be only in the mind, because it is possible to think of something which exists also in reality and that would be greater. If, therefore, that than which nothing greater can be conceived is only in the mind, that than which a greater cannot be conceived is that than which a greater can be conceived and this certainty cannot be. Consequently, without doubt, that than which nothing greater can be conceived exists both in the mind and in reality. This, then, is so sure that one cannot think of its not being so. For it is possible to think of something which one cannot conceive not to exist which is greater than that which can be thought not to exist. Consequently, if that a greater than which cannot be conceived can be thought not to exist, it is not that a greater than which cannot be conceived. But this does not make sense. Therefore, it is true that something than which a greater cannot be conceived is not able to be conceived as not existing. This art Thou, O Lord, my God.

C. To this the monk Gaunilo replied that it is possible to conceive of an island greater than any other island, but this does not prove that it exists. Anselm replied in the Liber Apolog. contra Gaunilonem, *iv.* P.L. *158, pp. 253-254.*

✔ ✔ ✔

Although whatever actually is cannot be thought of as not being, nevertheless all things can be conceived of as not being except the highest. For everything and only that can be thought of as not being which has beginning, end or conjunction of parts. Therefore, only of God can it be said that it is not possible to think of His not being.

D. Abelard's dialectical method. "Sic et non" P.L. *178, pp. 1340-1350, 1393 and 1367.*

✔ ✔ ✔

Inasmuch as among the multitudinous words of the saints there are some which are not only diverse, but actually adverse the one to the other, we are not to judge lightly of these saints who themselves will judge the world. . . . If there are divine mysteries which we cannot understand in the spirit in which they were written, better to reserve judgment than to define rashly. We are not to rely on apocryphal writings and we must be sure that we have the correct text of the canonical. For example, Matthew and John say that Jesus was crucified at the sixth hour, but Mark at the third. This is an error of transcription in

Mark. We are to observe that sometimes an author is in
error because he carelessly incorporated the work of
someone else, as Augustine confessed he had done with
reference to Origen. We must bear in mind the diversity
of situation in which particular sayings were utttered. In
case of controversy between the saints, which cannot be
resolved by reason, we should hold to that opinion which
has the most ancient and powerful authority. And if sometimes the fathers were in error we should attribute this
not to duplicity but ignorance, and if sometimes they were
absurd, we are to assume that the text is faulty, the interpreter in error or simply that we do not understand.

Therefore it has seemed to us fitting to collect from the
holy fathers apparently contradictory passages that tender
readers may be incited to make inquiry after the truth.
. . . By doubting we come to inquire, and by inquiry we
arrive at the truth. . . . We are including nothing from
the Apocrypha and nothing from the writings of Augustine which he later retracted.

Example XXXII. That God may do all things and
that He may not. Chrysostom said that God is called
almighty because it is impossible to find anything that
is impossible for Him. Nevertheless He cannot lie, or
be deceived, He cannot be ignorant, He cannot have a
beginning or an end. He cannot forget the past, be involved in the present or be ignorant of the future. Finally, He cannot deny Himself. Augustine said there are
some things God can do as to His power, but not as to His
justice. Being himself justice He cannot commit injustice.
He is omnipotent in the sense that He can do what He
wants. But He cannot die, He cannot change and He cannot be deceived.

Example XI. That the divine persons differ from each
other and that they do not.

Athanasius said there is one person of the Father, one
of the Son and one of the Holy Spirit. The Father is not
made, created or begotten. The Son comes solely from the
Father. He is not made or created but He is begotten. The
Spirit proceeds from the Father and the Son. He is not
begotten or created but proceeding. But Pope Leo I said,
"In the divine Trinity nothing is dissimilar, nothing un-
equal."

II. Mysticism

Bernard of Clairvaux on union with God. "De Dili-gendo Deo," *Select Treatises of St. Bernard, ed. W. Williams,* Cambridge Patristic Texts (*Cambridge, England, 1926*). *Chap. X.*

✤   ✤   ✤

O love, holy and chaste! O sweet and gracious affection! O pure and refined intent of the will, all the more pure and refined because in it remains no trace of itself, all the more gracious and sweet because what is felt is solely divine. So to be moved is to be deified. For just as a tiny drop immersed in a vessel of wine seems wholly to lose itself and to take on the savor and color of wine; just as iron heated to incandescence appears to lose utterly its pristine form and to be indistinguishable from fire, and just as air pierced by a sunbeam is so transformed into the very clarity of light as to seem not so much to be enlightened as to be light itself, so likewise in the saints every human affection needs in some ineffable manner to be dissolved from itself and completely transmuted into the will of God. For otherwise how shall God be all in all, if in man there remain anything of man? His substance will indeed remain, but in another form, another glory, another power. When then shall this take place? Who then will behold? Who will possess? When shall I come and appear before the face of God? O Lord, my God, my heart has spoken to Thee, my face has sought Thee. Thy face, Lord, do I seek.

III. The Cistercian Movement

Bernard's critique of Cluny. Apologia ad Guillelmum Sancti-Theodori Abbatem, P. L. *182, pp. 895-919.*

✤   ✤   ✤

To the venerable father William, Brother Bernard of the brethren at Citeaux, a useless servant, greetings in the Lord: When have I reviled the order of Cluny? When have I tried to persuade one of them to come over to us? I sent one back. There is room for more than one type of order like Mary and Martha. The Scripture says "At thy

right hand doth stand the queen in gold of Ophir and
girded with variety." [*Vulgate Ps. 45:9*]. Therefore the
diverse may follow the diverse, whether Cluniacs or Cistercians, seculars or regulars, clergy or laity etc. Am I a
Cistercian? Do I then damn the Cluniacs? God forbid!
But when I upbraid the defects of my own order let it
not be thought that I condone yours. I marvel that among
monks there should be such intemperance in eating and
drinking, in clothes, dormitories, stables and sumptuous
buildings. At Cluny frugality is called avarice, sobriety
is dubbed austerity, silence is moroseness. On the other
hand remissness is called discretion; prodigality is liberality, loquacity is affability, raucous laughter jocundity, soft
clothing and elegant horses constitute respectability. Extra
attention to bedding is called cleanliness. And when we
abet each other in these things, that is charity. O how far
are we fallen from the monks in the days of St. Anthony!
What shall I say of the use of water when you do not even
mix it with your wine? The apostle Paul allowed Timothy
a little wine for his stomach's sake [*I Tim. 5:23*]. So we
all have weak stomachs and forget that word *little*. And
what of mixing wine with honey and spices? Is that for
the weakness of the stomach? Because meat is allowed in
the infirmary we are all infirm, hobbling with canes to
make it appear that we are sick. Talk about clothes! Who
would spend 200 solidi to deck out a mule? You say that
religion is not in the habit, but in the heart. All right! But
whatever is coarse you reject, and whatever is splendid
you covet. Is that from the heart? You ask why, if these
practices are wrong, the abbots have not suppressed them.
I lie not if I have not seen an abbot with an equipage of
sixty horses. Will not a light shine without being set into
a candelabra of silver or gold? Will not one vessel do both
for washing hands and drinking wine? And is not one
servant enough to make a bed, tie a horse and serve a
table? I will pass over the immense height of churches, the
vast expanses, the superfluous breadth, the sumptuous dec-
orations and the curious depictions. I ask you devotees of
poverty, what has gold to do with a sanctuary? How are
our devotions aided by beautiful lights, ravishing melodies
and sweet odors? Men rather admire the beautiful than
adore the sacred. For candelabras we see trees standing

erect with the weight of the brass, marvelously fabricated not the less coruscating from the lights than from the gems. Do you think all this makes for the contrition of penitence? The church is refulgent in its walls and the poor suffer lack. She sets gems in her stones and leaves her sons naked. Do we revere the images of the saints when we put them into pavements and walk on them? Often we spit into the mouth of an angel. And why cannot we spare the sacred images the adornment of color? And what of these ridiculous monstrosities of deformed beauty and beautiful deformity? vile monkeys, fierce lions, monstrous centaurs, half men? What of the striped tigers? soldiers fighting, hunters blowing horns? Here you see a quadruped with a serpent's tail or a fish with the head of a quadruped and here a beast half horse, half goat. It is easier to read in marble than in codices. One could spend a whole day gaping instead of meditating on God. Good grief, what ineptidue! and what expense!

IV. The Beginning of Gothic Architecture

The Abbot Suger, "The Consecration of the Church of St. Denis," from the text in Erwin Panofsky, Abbot Suger *(Princeton, 1946).*

✓   ✓   ✓

The disparity of the human and the divine is equalized by the admirable power of the one singular and highest reason, and these disparates which appear to be utterly contrary on account of inferiority of origin and contrariety of nature, are conjoined solely by the gracious congruence of the one superior and tempered harmony. Thereby the internal strife of spirit and body is overcome. We are delivered from sensuality and the hampering of the exterior senses. Carnal desires are forgotten through the conjunction of the highest reason and eternal beatitude. Having then peace with God, after the manner of those who give token of gratitude, we have rendered an account of the consecration of this church and of the translation of the relics of our most precious patrons Denis, Rusticus and Eleutherius, that we may solemnly give thanks to divine grace and obtain the intercession of our holy protectors.

Our former church was constructed with royal munificence by the glorious and famous king of the Franks, Dagobert, who, in response to a vision of the saints, erected in their honor a basilica of marble adorned with jewels of incomparable splendor. In time this edifice became too small to accommodate the throngs who came to kiss the holy relics of the Lord, the nail and the crown of thorns. Such was the press that men were as immobile as statues, women took on the pallor of death and cried out as in travail and others, lifted by the men, crawled over them as on a pavement.

I knew not where to find marble for the new church and thought of bringing columns from the baths of Diocletian at Rome through the Mediterranean under convoy even of the Saracens, then by the English Sea and the tortuous Seine, when the Almighty revealed to us a quarry nearby at Pontoise. The columns were hauled by common folk and noble who alike harnassed themselves as beasts of burden. Similarly I knew not where to find adequate timber and supposed that it would be necessary to go to remote Auxerre. I resolved, however, to search the forest of Iveline. though told that it had already been stripped of larger timbers for fortifications. I penetrated the thickets and found twelve trees which the Lord Jesus had protected from the plunderers and reserved for Himself and the Holy Martyrs.

The plan was to build a new church and to integrate the old with the new, except for the gracious and laudable extension of a cluster of chapels by which the entire sanctuary should be suffused with a marvelous and perpetual light from the most holy windows, adding lustre to the beauty within.

Summer and winter for three years we labored and when the church was done we resolved to build a new reliquiary for the remains of our patron saints and in front of this to construct an altar, to which peers, princes and bishops sent precious stones and the illustrious king himself presented exquisite emeralds. The consecration was set for the second Sunday in June and was attended by our Lord King Louis, Queen Eleanor, the Queen Mother and divers peers, archbishops and bishops from France and the Archbishop of Canterbury. When the king and the nobility beheld the chorus of such pontiffs in white vestments with mitres, bejewelled orphreys and croziers, processing to celebrate the nuptials of the Eternal Spouse, to them it appeared that this was rather a heavenly than an earthly chorus, a ceremony less human than divine.

When the reliquiary executed under King Dagobert was opened and the bodies of the saints exposed, the king and all the nobles chanted and wept with joy unspeakable. The most Christian king received the silver chasse of our special patron and led the procession of those bearing candles and crosses. After the consecration of the main altar and of twenty others, a solemn mass was celebrated whose melody, ravishing in consonance and congruent harmony, seemed rather a heavenly than an earthly symphony, and all with one heart and voice acclaimed, "Blessing, honor and glory be unto Thy name, Lord Jesus Christ, (Rev. 5:13) whom God the Father hath anointed High Priest with the oil of gladness above Thy fellows. (Heb. 1:9, Ps. 45) By this most holy chrism and through reception of the most holy Eucharist Thou dost conjoin the corporeal with the spiritual, the human with the divine and through visible benedictions dost invisibly restore and wondrously transform this present into the celestial kingdom, through power and mercy making us and the angelic creature, both heaven and earth into one commonwealth, Thou who livest and reignest, God forever and ever, Amen."

— Reading No. 6 —

THE PEAK OF THE PAPACY

I. Innocent III on Church and State

A. The pope must endorse an imperial election. Decretal
Venerabilem Fratrem, *March 1202. Mirbt, No. 323.*

✓   ✓   ✓

We recognize that the authority and power to elect a
king to be an emperor appertains to the princes as of ancient custom, the more valid because the Roman Church
transferred the empire in the person of Charlemagne from
the Greeks to the Germans. But the princes ought to recognize, as they do, that the authority and right of examin-
ing the person elected to be promoted to the empire belongs to us, who anoint, consecrate and crown. It is
regularly and generally observed that the examination of
a person pertains to the one who has the laying on of
hands. Now, if the princes are not only in disaccord but
even if they are in concord, conspiring together to elect
a sacrilegious, excommunicated person, a tyrant, imbecile,
heretic or pagan, shall we then anoint, consecrate or
crown such a man? Absolutely not.

B. Spiritual and temporal jurisdiction. Per Venerabilem,
Sept.-Dec., 1202. Mirbt, No. 324.

✓   ✓   ✓

To William of Montpellier Through our venerable
brother, the archbishop of Arles, your Nobility has requested the legitimization of your sons lest there be any
defect in the succession. The authority of legitimization
does reside within the Roman Church not only in spirituals but also in temporals and you, unlike the king of
France, are subject to us in both because you hold part

of your territory from the church at Montpellier, which is subject in temporals to the Apostolic See. Nevertheless because you have not a good case (details given) we deny your request.

C. The Pope judges the sin, not the fief. Decretal Novit, *1204. Mirbt, No. 325.*

✓   ✓   ✓

He who is the searcher of hearts and from whom no secrets are hid, well knows that out of pure love and unfeigned conscience we cherish our distinguished son in Christ, Philip the King of France. We have no intention of diminishing or disturbing the jurisdiction or power of the illustrious king of France, as he ought not and does not desire to impede ours. Why should we who can hardly take care of our own jurisdiction, wish to usurp another's? But when the Lord says in the gospel that if an offending brother will not listen, you should take it to the church (Mt. 18:15) and the King of England affirms and is prepared to prove, that the King of France has offended against him and the procedure of the gospel has been followed to the point of bringing the case to the church, how then can we, who have been called by divine disposition to the pinnacle of the universal Church, fail to heed the divine mandate, unless reason to the contrary can be shown before us or our legate? We do not intend to judge concerning the feudal obligation, but concerning the sin, which without any doubt belongs to us. Although in the case of any offender we should seek to reclaim the sinner, recalling him from vice to virtue, from error to truth, especially must we do so when he sins against the peace, which is the bond of love.

D. The two lights. Sicut universitatis conditor. *Mirbt, No. 326.*

✓   ✓   ✓

As God the Creator of the universe established "two great lights in the firmament of heaven, the greater light to rule the day and the lesser light to rule the night"

(Gen. 1:16), so in the firmament of the universal Church which is called by the name of heaven, He established two great dignities, the greater which rules over souls, corresponding to the day, and the lesser to rule over bodies, corresponding to the night. These are the pontifical and the regal authorities. As the moon derives its light from the sun and is inferior both in quality and quantity, so the regal power derives the splendor of its dignity from the pontifical authority.

E. Transsubstantiation. Fourth Lateran Council, Cap. 1, De Fide Catholica. Mirbt, No. 329.

✓   ✓   ✓

There is one universal Church of the faithful outside of which none can be saved, in which Jesus Christ himself is the high priest and sacrifice, whose body and blood are truly contained in the sacrament of the altar under the species of bread and wine, the bread being transsubstantiated into the body and the wine into the blood by divine power so that for the perfecting of the mystery of the union we receive from his what he receives from ours. No one is able to perform this sacrament other than a priest rightly ordained according to the keys of the Church, which Jesus Christ confided to the apostles and their successors.

II. The Rise of Heresy

A. The Albigenses. Innocent III to the Archbishop of Narbonne, May 1203, P.L. 215, p. 83.

✓   ✓   ✓

I understand that the Apostolic See by special dispensation permitted you to enjoy the revenues both of the metropolis of Narbonne and of the abbey of Mount Aragon in the hope that you would reside in both and profit both, and not be entirely absent from either, but with grief we learn that you are present in both in a way that profits neither. Following the lusts of the flesh you neglect the pastoral office. The church of Narbonne is derelict. Residing in the abbey you treat all too tenderly those whom the flesh has endeared to you and show that you hate those whom love should have made more dear. . . . Ravening wolves invade the flock committed to you, raging the more against your sheep because like a dumb dog you do not bark. Neither do you frighten them off, nor like a good shepherd lay down your life for the sheep, but rather you flee. See then, because you neglect the work of God the little foxes invade the vines. The heretics, taking advantage of your absence, publically disseminate perverse dogmas in the province of Narbonne and a great multitude gives heed to them. Therefore, lest the Lord require their blood from your hand, if you continue in your neglect, we command your Fraternity by apostolic mandate and we stringently decree that either you leave absolutely the abbey of Mount Aragon and reside in the church of Narbonne, there worthily exercising your pastoral office, or that you be content, if you prefer, with the abbey and renounce the metropolitan dignity, for we are unwilling to sustain any longer such loss to the church of Narbonne or rather of the Christian people, and we ought not in any way to tolerate that the same church should suffer widowhood while you are alive, but if you are unwilling to perform the conjugal due, let some one else marry her [*the church*] who will console her in her extremity and purge her of heretical pravity.

B. The Waldenses. Walther Map, "De Nugis Curialium," Anecdota Oxoniensia, *Med. & Mod. Ser. XIV, ed. M. R. James (Oxford, 1914). Chap. xxxi, pp. 60-61.*

✓   ✓   ✓

In the Roman council under Pope Alexander III we saw Waldenses, simple and illiterate men, named after their leader Waldo, a citizen of Lyons on the Rhone. They submitted to the pope a book in French with the text and gloss on the Psalter. With great importunity they sought authorization to preach, since in their own eyes they appeared learned, though, as a matter of fact, barely scholars. Out of the many there present, learned in the law, I was commissioned to examine them. Two of the Waldenses, who appeared to be leaders in their sect, were brought before me to dispute concerning the faith, not out of love of the truth on their part, but that they might close my mouth as one speaking iniquity. I confess I was nervous. The pope ordered me to contend against them.

First then I proposed the very simplest question: "Do you believe in God the Father?" They replied, "We believe." "And in the Son?" Again, "We believe." "And in the Holy Ghost?" Once more, "We believe." "And in the Mother of Christ?" Again they said, "We believe." Whereupon every one present broke into a roar of derisive laughter, and they retired in confusion, as well they might. [*What they ought to have answered was, "The Mother of God." Their answer savored of the old Nestorian heresy.*] These people have no fixed abodes. Two by two they go about barefoot, clad in wool, having nothing, holding all things in common, naked following the naked Christ.

III. The Inquisition

Tractatus de Haeresi Paupertatum de Lugduno, *ed. Edmund Martène*, Thesaurus Novus Anecdotorum (*Paris, 1717*), *V, pp. 1789-1790.*

✓   ✓   ✓

When one of [*the heretics*] is brought for examination he comes in nonchalantly as if aware of nothing amiss. Then I ask him why he has been summoned. He says meekly and blandly, "Sir, I'd like to know from you." I say, "You are accused of being a heretic and of believing other than as the holy Church believes and teaches." Raising his eyes to heaven he replies with great confidence, "Lord, Thou knowest I am innocent of this and have never held any faith other than the true Christian faith." I say, "You call your faith Christian, because you consider ours to be false and heretical, but I adjure you to say whether you have ever taught or believed as true any faith other than that of the Roman Church." He says, "The faith which the Church holds, that I hold to be true." I say, "Do you not have some fellow sectaries whom you call the Holy Church whose faith you believe?" He replies, "The true faith which the Roman Church believes and which you publicly preach to us, that I believe." I say, "But perhaps as you have at Rome some of your sect whom you call the Roman Church and you hold their faith. When I preach I say numerous things and on some points we are in accord, as that there is a living God, and so you believe some of what I preach. Nevertheless you may be a heretic if you do not accept other points which also ought to be believed." He answers, "I believe every-thing which a Christian ought to believe." I say, "I know your tricks, because, as I said, you believe that the points to be believed by a Christian are those of your sect. But we waste time with this sparring. Say simply; Do you be-lieve in one God the Father, and Son and Holy Spirit?" He answers promptly, "I believe." "Do you believe in Christ born of the Virgin, suffered, risen from the dead and ascended into heaven?" He answers with alacrity, "I believe." "Do you believe the bread and the wine, when the priest celebrates the mass, to be changed by divine power, into the body of Christ?" He answers, "Ought I not to believe this?" I say, "I do not ask whether you ought to believe but whether you do." He responds, "I believe whatever you and other good Christians order me to believe." I say, "Those good doctors with whom you wish to believe are the leaders of your sect, with whom if I believe, then you believe with me, but otherwise not." He answers, "I gladly believe with you if you teach me what is good." I say, "You consider that good which your masters teach. Come now, do you believe that the body of the Lord Jesus Christ is on the altar?" He answers promptly, "I believe." I say, "You know that a body is there and all bodies are of the Lord. I ask whether there is on the altar the body of the Lord which was born of the Virgin, hung on the cross, rose and ascended." He answers, "And you, Sir, do you not believe it?" I say, "I believe it entirely." He answers, "I likewise believe." I say, "You believe that I believe, which is not what I ask but whether you believe?" He replies, "If you twist every-thing that I say I don't know what to answer. I am a simple man. Don't try to catch me in my words." I say, "If you are a simple man answer simply without any equivocation." He says, "Gladly." "Will you then swear that you have never taught anything contrary to the faith which we hold to be true?" Turning pale he answers, "If I ought to swear I will gladly swear." I say, "I don't ask you whether you ought but whether you will." He answers, "If you order me to swear I will swear." I say, "I don't com-pel you to swear. Because you consider oaths unlawful, you will cast the blame on me. But if you will swear I will hear you." He answers, "But why should I swear if you do not order me?" I say, "In order that you may remove the suspicion of heresy." He answers, "Sir, I do not know how unless you teach me." I say, "If I were going to swear I would raise my hand, extend the fingers as is customary and say, 'So help me God, I have never taught heresy nor believed anything contrary to the true faith.'" Then trembling, and as if he did not know the form of the words, he will stumble and garble the words, perhaps turning the oath into the form of a prayer and end up by saying, "Didn't you hear me swear?" I have heard all of these questions and answers from converted heretics who disclose the evasions employed in the interrogation.

IV. The New Monasticism. St. Francis on the perfect joy. Translated from I Fioretti di San Francesco, *ed. Adolfo Padovan (1915), Ch. viii. Slightly reduced.*

St. Francis was once traveling with Brother Leo from Perugia to Saint Mary of the Angels. The time was winter and excruciatingly cold. St. Francis called to Brother Leo, who was somewhat ahead, and said, "Brother Leo, if the Friars Minor should go to all parts of the earth and give a noble and edifying example of holy living, write and note well that not here would be the perfect joy." Then after a while a second time he called, "O Brother Leo, if a Friar Minor were to give sight to the blind, make the crooked straight, cast out demons, make the deaf to hear, the lame to walk, the dumb to speak and raise the dead after four days, write that in this is not the perfect joy." Then, after a little, again he cried loudly, "O Brother Leo, if the Friar Minor knew all the languages, all the sciences, all the Scriptures, and were able not only to disclose the secrets of the future but to read the inmost thoughts of the soul, write that in this is not the perfect joy." Then once more, after a bit, even more loudly he cried, "O Brother Leo, lambkin of God, if the Friar Minor could speak with the tongue of an angel and knew the courses of the stars and the virtues of the herbs, if all the treasures of the earth were revealed to him and he knew the quality of the birds, the fish, of all animals and man, of trees, stones, roots and water, write that in this is not the perfect joy." And then still again in a loud voice, "O Brother Leo, if the Friar Minor could so preach as to convert all the infidels to the faith of Christ, write that not herein is the perfect joy." When they had gone on in this fashion for some two miles Brother Leo, in great amazement, exclaimed, "Well, for God's sake, Father, tell me where it is then." And St. Francis answered, "When we arrive at Saint Mary of the Angels, drenched with rain, congealed with cold, smeared with mud and faint with hunger, and knock at the door and the porter comes out and says, 'Who are you?' and we say, 'We are two of your friars,' and he says, 'You are nothing of the sort. You are two rogues who go about deceiving the world and robbing the poor of their alms. Get out of here,' and he makes us stand outside famished in the snow until night . . . and if then, constrained by hunger and cold and the night, we plead with him, for the love of God, to let us in, but instead he comes with a cudgel, grabs us by the cowls, knocks us down in the snow, beats every bone and we endure with patience and joy, thinking of the pangs of the blessed Christ, which we also should bear for love of him, write, Brother Leo, that here and in this is the perfect joy."

— Reading No. 7 —

THE FAITH

I. Formulation

A. Thomas Aquinas on faith and reason. Summa Contra Gentiles, *Book I, ch. 4-8. Text Petri Fiaccadori (Parma, 1852-73; photolith New York, 1948).*

✦   ✦   ✦

iv) If the sole way of knowing God were through reason the human mind would remain in the deepest shadows of ignorance. The provision of divine providence was therefore wholesome that those truths which reason is able to investigate should none the less be held by faith.

v) Because men are ordained by divine providence for a higher good than human frailty can express in the present life, the mind is summoned to something higher than our reason here and now can reach. For then only do we know God truly when we believe Him to be above everything which man can conceive concerning Him.

vii) Nevertheless, although the above mentioned truth of the Christian faith exceeds the capacity of human reason, still those conclusions which are naturally indited by reason cannot be contrary to this truth, for those propositions which are naturally instilled are so very true that it is not possible to think of them as false. Nor can we regard as false that which is manifestly communicated from on high.

viii) The role of human reason with reference to knowing the truth of faith, which is fully clear only to those who behold the divine substance, is to collect certain similitudes resembling it. These do not suffice by way of demonstration or comprehension of this truth through themselves. Nevertheless, that the human mind should be exercised in such reasonings, however feeble, is useful, provided there be no presumptuous claim of comprehension or demonstration.

B. The doctrine of the seven sacraments. Eugenius IV, Exultate Deo, *Nov. 22, 1439. Mirbt, No. 401.*

✔   ✔   ✔

In the Christian dispensation there are seven sacraments: baptism, confirmation, the Eucharist, penance, extreme unction, ordination and marriage which both contain grace and confer it upon those who receive worthily. The first five refer to the spiritual perfection of each man in himself. The last two apply to the administration and expansion of the entire Church. By baptism we are spiritually reborn. By confirmation we are increased in grace and strengthened in faith. Being thus reborn and fortified we are nourished by the divine nutriment of the eucharist. If through sin we fall into weakness of the soul we are cured spiritually by penance. Extreme unction is of benefit spiritually and corporally so far as is expedient for the soul. Through ordination the Church is truly governed and spiritually multiplied and through matrimony is augmented in the flesh. These sacraments are affected in three ways, by things as to their material, by words as to their form and by the person of the one officiating as to the intention to do what the Church does. If any one of these is lacking the sacrament is not complete. Among these sacraments there are three, baptism, confirmation and ordination, which imprint upon the soul an indelible character. Therefore they are not to be repeated on the same person. The other four do not confer an indelible character and may be repeated.

The first place among the sacraments is held by baptism. The matter of the sacrament is true and natural water, whether hot or cold. The form is, "I baptize in the name of the Father and of the Son and of the Holy Ghost." [*Some variation is allowed provided the Trinity be mentioned.*] The minister of this sacrament is a priest, but in case of necessity the rite may be performed by a deacon, layman, a woman or even a pagan or a heretic, provided he uses the form of the Church and intends to do what the Church does. The effect of this sacrament is the remission of original and actual sin and the removal of all penalty so that no satisfaction is to be enjoined for sins committed prior to baptism. Those who die before having committed any sin go straight to heaven and enjoy the vision of God. The second sacrament is confirmation. The matter is chrism of oil, signifying excellence of conscience, and balsam blessed by the bishop, signifying the odor of a good reputation. The form is, "I sign you with the sign of the cross and confirm you with the chrism of salvation in the name of the Father and of the Son and of the Holy Ghost." This sacrament is to be administered only by a bishop. Its effect is to confer the Holy Spirit.

The third is the sacrament of the Eucharist, whose sign is wheaten bread and wine from the vine with which before consecration a little water may be mixed. The form of the sacrament is the words of the Savior at the institution. The priest in the person of Christ speaking administers the sacrament. By virtue of the words themselves the substance of bread is converted into the body of Christ and the substance of wine into the blood, but in such fashion that the whole of Christ is present in each element.

The effect is that whatever food and drink can do for the body by way of sustenance, increase, restoration and delight, this the sacrament does for the spiritual life. The fourth sacrament is penance whose material part is the act of penitence in three components. The first is contrition of the heart, the second confession of the mouth by which all sins remembered are to be confessed to the priest completely. The third is satisfaction for sins according to the judgment of the priest particularly through prayer, fasting and alms. The form of this sacrament is in the words of absolution *Ego te absolvo*. The minister is the priest. The effect is absolution from sins.

The fifth is extreme unction whose matter is olive oil blessed by the bishop. This sacrament is to be given only to those whose death appears imminent. The anointing is to be applied to the eyes, ears, nose, mouth, hands, feet and reins. The form is: "By this holy anointing and by His most holy mercy may God grant unto you that . . ." The minister is the priest. The effect is the healing of the mind and if it be expedient of the body.

The sixth is ordination. The material in the case of the priest (not of the deacon) is the offering of a chalice of wine and a paten of bread. The form for a priest is: "Accept the power to offer sacrifice in the Church for the living and the dead in the name of the Father and of the Son and of the Holy Ghost." The bishop officiates. The effect is an increase in grace to become a worthy minister.

The seventh is matrimony. The efficient cause is consent expressed by words in person. There are three goods of marriage. The first is the bearing and rearing of children in the worship of God. The second is faith by which each partner should serve the other. The third is indissolubility after the manner of the indissoluble union of Christ and the Church. There may be separation because of fornication but the marriage is not dissolved.

II. Expression: The Plight of Man

A. The First Lullaby in the English tongue, published by Carleton Brown, Religious Lyrics of the Fourteenth Century *(Oxford, 1924), No. 28, modernized by R.H.B.*

Lollai, lollai, little child, why weepest thou so sore?
Needs must thou weep, it was ordained of yore
Ever to live in sorrow and sigh and mourn ever,
As thine elders did ere this, while they alivéd were.
Lollai, lollai, little child, child, lollai, lullow,
Into uncouth world i-comen so art thou.

Beastes and those fowls, the fishes in the flood
And each living thing, i-made of bone and blood,
When he cometh to the world he doth himself some
    good—
All but the wretched child that is of Adam's blood.
Lollai, lollai, little child, by care art thou beset.
Thou knowest nought this world's wild before thee is
    set.
Child if betideth that thou shalt goodly be
Think thou wert fostered upon thy mother's knee;
Ever have mind in thy heart of those things three:
Whence thou comest, where thou art and what shall
    come of thee.
Lollai, lollai, little child, child, lollai, lollai.
With sorrow thou come into this world,
With sorrow shalt thou wend away.

B. The Day of Doom. Thomas of Celano. Dies Irae, *text
in J. S. Phillimore,* Hundred Best Latin Hymns *(London,
1926), No. 92.*

Day of dolor, direful ill
Will the world in flames distill,
Witness David and Sybil.

What a tremor and a quaking
When the Judge, His ire awaking,
All things swiftly will be shaking.

At the trumpet's strident tone
The dead will rise up bone for bone
To be herded round the throne.

Death and nature will despond
When the creatures break their bond,
At the judgment to respond.

When the Judge enthroned is sighted,
Hidden things will then be lighted
And the unavenged requited.

Oh, how smitten shall I fall!
On what patron shall I call,
When not the just is sure at all?

King of utter majesty,
Whose redemptive gift is free,
Save, oh save, oh save Thou me.

Forget not, oh Thou Jesus dear,
I am the cause that Thou wast here,
To save me from this frightful fear.

To find me erring Thou wast fain,
To redeem me Thou was slain.
Let not Thy labor be in vain.

Judge, whose judgments all are fit,
Wilt Thou not my guilt remit
Before I am accused of it?

I blush and tremble for my guilt,
For I have trespassed to the hilt,
Oh God, save me if Thou wilt.

Like Mary Magdalene forgiven
And the thief with Thee in heaven,
May I also now be shriven.

Save me from the goats rejected,
Set me with the sheep selected,
On Thy right no more dejected.

When Thou dost the bad confound,
And in acrid flames impound
May Thy grace to me abound.

Suppliant to Thee I bow.
Contrite heart to Thee I vow.
Deign to save me here and now.

C. 1. The Work of Redemption: "Sunset on Calvary," the title given to a thirteenth-century English lyric by Carleton Brown in English Lyrics of the Thirteenth Century (*Oxford, 1932*), *No. 1, modernized by R.H.B.*

✔   ✔   ✔

[*To the Virgin*]
Now sinks the sun behind the glade.
I sorrow for thy face, fair maid.
Now sinks the sun behind the tree.
I sorrow for thy Son and thee.

C. 2. The Stabat Mater, *Text in Phillimore,* op. cit., No. 95.

✔   ✔   ✔

Stood the stricken Mother weeping
By the cross her vigil keeping
While they crucified the Lord.
Grievously her heart was riven
To whom the word had once been given
She should be piercéd by a sword.

Who is he who would not mourn
To see Christ's Mother so forlorn
Smitten by his bitter pang?
Who would not lament and wail,
As he saw her, would not quail?
Anguished to behold him hang?

For the wrongs by mankind done
Saw she the suffering of her Son,
Scourged and nailéd to a tree,
Saw the sweet Son of her womb
Dying in the deepest gloom
With a cry of agony.

Oh thou fount of love in sorrow
Give to me the grace to follow,
That with thee my heart may suffer.
Fire my soul with such a burning
That my steps to Christ returning
He to me his grace may proffer.

By his nail prints lacerated,
By his cross inebriated,
May I in his blood be laved.
Grant that I who have offended
Be by thee the Maid defended,
And from the fire of judgment saved.

When, Oh Christ, I come to die
Through her protecting grace may I
Receive the palm of victory,
And when my flesh enterréd lies
May my soul in paradise
In glory dwell for ayé in thee.

D. The Bliss of Paradise: Abelard, O Quanta, qualia.
Phillimore, op. cit., *No. 37.*

How wondrous the sabbaths to which we aspire,
Eternally kept by the heavenly choir;
Repose for the weary, a crown for the brave,
When God the Almighty shall have swallowed the
    grave!

Jerusalem truly betokens that state
Whose peace and jocundity naught can abate,
Where fulfillment is never outrun by desire
Nor desire can cause the reward to retire.

What king! what court! what palace! what peace!
What rest! what joy without any surcease!
Let them tell what they feel, if tell it they can
Who share in the glory made known unto man.

Ours, while we journey, to lift up our eyes
To seek our true country with yearning and sighs;
From Babylon flee, as Jerusalem calls
That after long exile we return to her walls.

Songs there secure of Zion we shall sing,
No longer molested by aught baneful thing.
Perpetual praise for the gifts of Thy grace
Thy people present, O Lord, to Thy face.

There sabbath on sabbath the symphony swells
Of joy never ending on sweet chiming bells.
Ineffable paeans ascend unto Thee.
And who are the singers? The angels and we.

III. Acquaintance with the Bible

A. St. Aelred, who became prior of Rievaulx in Yorkshire in 1141, a great friend of St. Bernard. The invocation of The Mirror of Love, *Bk. 1, Ch. 1, P.L. 195.*

❧   ❧   ❧

O Lord, Thou has spread out thy heavens as a garment, placing in them the stars that they may lighten us this night, in which the beasts of the forest rove, the young lions roaring for their prey and seeking their food from God. Thou makest the springs gush forth upon the hills that by the most secret cataracts Thou shouldst water the valleys of our hearts, making them to abound in wheat, wine and oil, that we sweat not in vain for our bread, but that seeking we may find, finding we may feed and taste how sweet art Thou, O Lord. My soul arid, sterile and barren thirsts to be flooded with these sweetest drops, that it may taste of that celestial bread on which angels feed and infants suck, that I may savor in my soul every delight, and no longer sigh for the flesh-pots which I left behind in Egypt, when Pharoah required bricks to be made without straw. Let thy voice, good Jesus, sound in my ears that it may show how my heart should love thee, how my mind should love thee, how the bowels of my soul should love thee. May my very marrow embrace thee, my sole good, my sweet and entrancing joy. [*The Biblical references are: Ps. 104:2, 21, 10; Gen. 3:19; Mt. 7:7; Ps. 34:8; Exod. 16:15; 16:3 and 5:7.*]

B. Richard Aungerville, known as Richard de Bury, was the bishop of Durham from 1287 to 1345. Having been sent by Edward III on a mission to Pope John XXII at Avignon, Richard reported that he might have utilized his errand to enrich himself with plush prebends, but he "preferred paltry pamphlets to pampered palfreys." On his return he wrote the Philobiblon *in praise of books. The*

*concluding section of his apostrophe to books is lush with
Biblical allusions, which are listed in order at the bottom
of the following translation made from the Latin text
edited by Ernest C. Thomas,* The Philobiblon *of Richard
de Bury (New York, 1889). The opening lines indulge in
word play on* libri, *books,* liberi, *free, and* liberales, *boun-
teous.*

O books, ye alone are free and freely do bestow. To
those who ask ye give and free your devoted slaves. By
how many thousands of learned men are ye commended
figuratively in the Scripture inspired of God! Ye are the
mines of profoundest wisdom to which the wise man in
Proverbs sends his son that thence he may dig treasures.
Ye are the wells of living waters which father Abraham
first dug and Isaac dug over again as often as the Philis-
tines filled them up. Ye are the luxuriant stalks full of ears
to be rubbed only by the hands of the apostles that food
may thence be milled for gracious and hungry souls. Ye
are the golden urns in which the manna was stored, rocks
flowing with honey, yea rather the very honey comb,
udders streaming with the milk of life, garners ever full.
Ye are the tree of paradise and the fourfold stream, by
which the human mind is pastured and the arid intellect
moistened and bedewed. Ye are the ark of Noah and the
ladder of Jacob, the watering troughs [*in which the striped
rods were set*] that the pregnant ewes viewing them might
bring forth striped kids. Ye are the stones of testimony,
the pitchers which held the lamps of Gideon, the pouch of
David holding the smooth stones for the slaying of Goli-
ath. Ye are the golden vessels of the temple, the shields of
the Christian soldier to withstand the poisonous darts of
the evil one. Fruitful olives, are ye, the vineyards of
Engedi, figs that know not to be barren, lamps burning and
ever in readiness— Yea, all the best in Scripture we might
apply to books if we chose to speak in figures. [*The Biblical references are: Prov. 2:4; Gen. 25:15-18; Mt. 12:1;
Lk. 6:1; Heb. 9:4; Dt. 32:13; Ex. 3:8; Mt. 3:12; Gen.
2:9-10; Gen. 6:14; Gen. 28:12; Gen. 30:38; Ex. 39:7; Jud.
7:16;* I *Sam. 17:40;* I *Kg. 7:48; Eph. 6:16; Dt. 8:8; Cant.
1:14; Mt. 21:19; Mt. 12:1-12. The reference to the streaming udders is from Virgil's* Fourth Eclogue]

IV. Dissemination through Preaching

The first example is from G. R. Owst, Literature and Pulpit in Medieval England *(Cambridge, England, 1933), pp. 300-301. The remaining three are from Ray C. Petry,* No Uncertain Sound *(Philadelphia, 1948), pp. 132, 156-157, 180-189.*

A. The plaint of the despoiled, from The Handbook of Bromyard.

✓　　　✓　　　✓

With boldness at the last judgment will they be able to put their plaint before God and seek justice, speaking with Christ the judge, and reciting each in turn the injury from which they specially suffered. Some of them were able to say, as the subjects of evil lords—"We have hungered. But those our lords standing over there were the cause of this, because they took us from our labors and our goods." Others—"We have hungered and died of famine, and those yonder did detain our goods that were owing to us." Others—"We have thirsted and been naked, because those standing opposite, each in his own way, so impoverished us that we were unable to buy drink and clothing." Others —"We were made infirm. Those yonder did it, who beat us and afflicted us with blows." Others—"We were without shelter. But those men were the cause of it, by driving us from our home and from our land; . . . or because they did not receive us into their own guesthouses." Others —"We were in prison. But those yonder were the cause, indicting us on false charges, and setting us in the stocks." Others—"Our bodies have not been buried in consecrated ground. Those yonder are responsible for this, by slaying us in numerous and various places. Avenge, O Lord, our blood that has been shed."

Bromyard adds: Without a doubt the just judge will do justice to those clamouring thus. Terrible as is the indictment of the wronged, terrible likewise will be the fate of the oppressors. Many who were here on earth called nobles shall blush in deepest shame at that Judgment-seat, when around their necks they shall carry, before all the

world, all the sheep and oxen and the beasts of the field
that they confiscated or seized and did not pay for.

B. The foolishness of the cross: Raoul Ardent.

✓   ✓   ✓

God hid His divine power in human weakness, and His
wisdom in foolishness. For to men it has seemed foolishness that God became man, that the Impassible suffered,
that the Immortal died. Therefore, the wisdom of God,
by foolishness, conquered the craft of the Devil. Let us,
therefore, brethren, learn from the example of our Redeemer to conquer the evil of this world, not by pride, but
by humility, by patience, and gentleness. Let us learn to
conquer the wisdom of this age, not by craftiness, but by
the foolishness of God. For indeed, to this age it seems
foolish and futile to despise the world, to reject the age,
to forsake all things, to love poverty and inferior station,
to desire things invisible. And yet, this foolishness con-
quers the wisdom of both the devil and man.

C. Contemplation and holiness: Bernard of Clairvaux.

✓   ✓   ✓

Does it appear to you that two persons have equal and
similar love towards Christ of whom the one sympathizes
indeed piously with his sufferings, is moved to a lively
sorrow by them and easily softened by the memory of all
that he endured; who feeds upon the sweetness of that
devotion, and is strengthened thereby to all salutary, hon-
ourable, and pious actions; while the other, being always
fired by a zeal for righteousness, having everywhere an
ardent passion for truth, and earnestly desiring wisdom
prefers above all things sanctity of life, and a perfectly
disciplined character; who is ashamed of ostentation, abhors detraction, knows not what it is to be envious, detests
pride, and not only avoids, but dislikes and despises every
kind of worldly glory; who vehemently hates and per-
severes in destroying in himself every impurity of the
heart and of the flesh; and lastly, who rejects, as if it were
naturally, all that is evil, and embraces all that is good?
If you compare these two types of affection, does it not
appear to you that the second is plainly the superior?

D. The ineffable joys of the celestial city chanted by Bede the Venerable.

✓   ✓   ✓

O truly blessed Mother Church! So illuminated by the honour of Divine condescension, so adorned by the glorious blood of triumphant martyrs, so decked with the inviolate confession of snow-white virginity! Among its flowers, neither roses nor lilies are wanting. Endeavor, now, beloved, each for yourselves, in each kind of honour, to obtain your own dignity—crowns, snow-white for chastity, or purple for passion.

With how joyous a breast the heavenly city receives those that return from fight! How happily she meets them that bear the trophies of the conquered enemy! With triumphant men, women also come, who rose superior both to this world and to their sex, doubling the glory of their warfare; virgins with youths, who surpassed their tender years by their virtues. Yet not they alone, but the rest of the multitude of the faithful shall also enter the palace of that eternal court, who in peaceful union have observed the heavenly commandments, and have maintained the purity of the faith.

— Reading No. 8 —

REALIGNMENTS

I. Heightening papal claims in the thirteenth century
A. Innocent IV, Eger, cui levia, end of 1245. Mirbt, No. 358.

✓   ✓   ✓

Those who assert that the Apostolic See initially obtained the primacy of empire from Constantine have not properly investigated the origins. For our Lord Jesus Christ, true man and true God, is both a true king and a true

priest after the order of Melchisedek. This plainly appears
in that sometimes he exercises for men the regalia of
majesty and sometimes the dignity of the priesthood in
pleading with the Father. This Christ has bestowed upon
the Apostolic See not only the pontifical but also the royal
majesty, conferring upon the blessed Peter and his successors the government at once of the earthly and of the
celestial empire. This is indicated by the use of the plural
keys, showing that as the vicar of Christ he has received
the power of rendering judgment, by the one key in temporals on earth and by the other in spirituals in heaven.
Truly Constantine, having been incorporated by faith into
the Church, humbly resigned to her the illegitimate tyranny which he had formerly exercised, and then received
from the vicar of Christ, the successor of Peter, the power
of rulership ordained of God that he should henceforth
punish the bad and vindicate the good, now legitimately
using the power which hitherto he had abused. Within the
bosom of the Church of the faithful the two swords of
the dual administration are included. When the Lord told
Peter to put up his sword he did not tell him to throw it
away, but to put it back in the scabbard and not to use it
any further to defend the Master, but he referred to "your
sword" and "your scabbard" to show that, although the
execution of this sword was not definitely interdicted to
him, nevertheless the authority of its actual use should
rest with the minister of the law to punish the bad and
protect the good. The material power of the sword is
implicit in the Church, but explicit in the emperor, who
receives it thence, and that which is only potential in the
bosom of the Church becomes actual when transferred to
the prince. The rite of coronation shows that the high
priest in conferring the crown puts the sword into the
scabbard. The prince as he receives and wields it acknowl-
edges that he has received it.

B. *Thomas Aquinas on the authority of the pope.*

1. Opusculum contra errores Graecorum ad Urbanum
IV. *Mirbt, No. 361.*

✓   ✓   ✓

By the authority of the aforementioned doctors it is
held that the Roman pontiff should have the plenitude of

power in the Church; again that Peter is the vicar of Christ and the Roman pontiff the successor of Peter enjoying the same power conferred upon him by Christ. A canon of the Council of Chalcedon says that if any bishop is accused he has the free right of appeal to the blessed bishop of ancient Rome since in Peter we have a rock of refuge. In accord with the keys bestowed on him by the Lord he alone has the free power in the place of God to pass judgment on bishops under accusation. Further it is plain that it is necessary for salvation to be subject to the Roman pontiff.

2. Summa Theol. *Sec. sec. q. 1*, De Fide. *Mirbt, No. 362.*

✼   ✼   ✼

As the highest pontiff is the head of the whole Church instituted by Christ, to him especially it pertains to set forth the symbol of the faith and to convene a general synod. The issuing of an edition of the symbol pertains to his authority whose right it is to determine finally those things which are of the faith. Paul said, "Let there not be schisms among you" [*I Cor. 1:10*], which cannot be unless when a question of faith arises it be settled by him who presides over the whole Church. Therefore to the sole authority of the highest pontiff belongs the issuing of a new symbol, as do all other things which pertain to the whole Church, such as the convening of a general synod and the like.

II. The clash of the Papacy with the French Monarchy

A. Boniface VIII. Clericis Laicos, *Feb. 25, 1296. Mirbt, No. 369.*

✼   ✼   ✼

To the clergy the laity have always been a thorn as antiquity relates and the present manifestly declares, for not being content with their bounds they invade the forbidden and fail to recognize that power over clerics, ecclesiastical persons and their goods is interdicted to them. Instead they impose grievous burdens on ecclesiastics both regular and secular, oppressing them with taillages and collections, exacting from their produce and goods a half, a tenth, a twentieth or whatever other portion of quota they exact or

extort, molesting them with multifarious services and subjecting them to their domination. Most sadly we note that
some prelates and ecclesiastical personages, trembling
where they have no business to tremble, seeking transitory
peace, fearing rather to offend temporal than eternal majesty, acquiesce in such abuses, not brashly but heedlessly
and without having obtained authorization from the Holy
See. We, therefore, desiring to correct these abuses, by
apostolic authority and the counsel of our brethren, decree that whatever prelates or ecclesiastical persons, regular or secular, of whatever order, condition or status,
shall pay, or promise or consent to pay to the laity collections, taillages, a tenth, a twentieth or a hundredth of
their own or the Church's produce or goods or any other
quantity, portion or quota . . . and that any emperors,
kings or princes, dukes, counts, barons, podestas, cap-
tains, officials or rectors, who impose, exact or receive
such levies and all who wittingly render them aid, counsel or favor, open or secret, shall thereby incur the sen-
tence of excommunication. Universities likewise, which
are culpable in this regard, are subject to ecclesiastical
censure. No one shall be absolved from the above mentioned excommunications and interdicts save in the hour
of death, without authority and special license from the
Apostolic See, for we are firmly resolved by no means to
pass over through dissimulation such atrocious abuse on
the part of the secular powers.

B. Boniface VIII, Unam Sanctam, *Nov. 18, 1302. Mirbt,
No. 372.*

One holy, Catholic and apostolic Church we are ur-
gently compelled by the faith to confess and hold and we
do believe and simply confess that outside of this Church
there is neither salvation nor the remission of sins. At the
time of the flood there was one ark of Noah, prefiguring
the Church, outside of which all that breathed upon the
earth perished. Of this ark there was one ruler, Noah.
This Church is the seamless robe of Christ, not to be rent.
Of this one and only Church there is one body and one
head, not two as if it were a monster. Christ is the head,
and Peter his vicar and Peter's succcessor, for the Lord

said to Peter, "Feed my sheep." He used the word "my" in a general sense, implying that all universally are committed to him. If, then, the Greeks or others say they are not committed to Peter and his successors they necessarily confess that they are not of the sheep of Christ, for the Lord said in John's gospel, "There is one flock and one shepherd" (21:17).

The gospels teach us that in the power of this shepherd there are two swords, the spiritual and the temporal, for when the apostles said, "Here are two swords," the Lord did not say, "This is too much," but "This is enough." Those who deny the temporal power to Peter do not carefully consider the word of the Lord, "Put your sword into the scabbard." Each sword, the spiritual and the material, is in the power of the Church, but the one is used by the Church, the other for the Church. The one is wielded by priests, the other by kings and soldiers, but at the behest of the priest. The sword needs to be under the sword, the temporal authority to be subject to the spiritual. For, when the apostle said, "The powers that be are ordained of God," he made it plain that they are not ordained unless they are ordered, the sword under the sword, as the blessed Dionysius says that the law of divinity is that the lowest through the intermediary is brought to the highest. . . . We must the more obviously confess that the spiritual excels the earthly in dignity and nobility to the degree that the spiritual is more excellent than the temporal. If, then, the earthly power errs it is to be judged by the spiritual; if the inferior spiritual power errs it is to be judged by its superior and if the supreme power errs it can be judged only by God, but not by man. For this authority, although given to man and exercised by man, is not human, but given by the divine mouth to Peter and his successors, to Peter called the rock, to whom the Lord said, "Whatsoever you shall bind, etc." (Mt. 16:19). Whoever, then, resists this power ordained by God resists the ordinance of God. . . . We, therefore, define, declare and pronounce that every human being to be saved must be subject to the Roman pontiff.

III. Getting, Spending and Giving

A. Provisions. In the late fourteenth century the University of Oxford wrote to the pope beseeching him to grant

*a provision for one of their scholars. Their petition is re-
produced in W. A. Pantin,* The English Church in the
Fourteenth Century *(Cambridge, England, 1955) from*
Oxford Formularies *II, p. 266.*

⨎   ⨎   ⨎

In the garden of the Church Militant, among other
fruit-bearing trees, God's providence with perpetual con-
stancy has rooted the Tree of Knowledge; the sweetness
of whose fruit the faithful in the Church taste every day,
when with aroused devotion they are healthfully instructed
by catholic doctors in the observance of the Divine law.
But lest, for lack of watering, such a health-giving tree
should at any time wither away with dried up branches;
from the seat of Your Holiness a certain foundation of
affluent grace is known to spring, by God's institution, so
that from it a river, coming out as it were from the paradise of pleasure, may everywhere fertilize the Church's
garden of delights with unfailing fruitfulness. Since therefore our beloved in Christ A. de B., divinely propagated
from the fruitful stock of the Sacred Page, an egregious
doctor, an excellent preacher, serene both in the purity of
his conscience and the honesty of his morals, has not as
much of the richness of the earth as the vigor of such
branches demands; therefore prostrate at the feet of Your
Beatitude, we humbly implore the clemency of Your Holiness, that having regard to the merits of the said colleague,
a river of grace may flow out from the apostolic plenitude,
to the relief of his indigence: mercifully deign to make
provision for him, if You please, in the church of York,
so that while he is watered by the dew of Your munificent
liberality, he may more abundantly bear fruit for others
unto salvation.

*B. The Statue of Provisors, A.D. 1390, 13 Richard II,
Stat. 2, from Gee & Hardy,* Documents Illustrative of
English Church History *(London, 1886), No. XXXIX.*

⨎   ⨎   ⨎

[*The act begins by a review of earlier legislation.*]
And now it is shown to our lord the king in this present
Parliament holden at Westminster, on the Octave of the
Purification of Our Lady, the five-and-twentieth year of
his reign of England, and the twelfth of France, by the

grievous complaint of all the common of his realm, that the grievances and mischiefs aforesaid do daily abound, to the greater damage and destruction of all the realm of England, more than ever were before, viz. that now anew our holy father the pope, by procurement of clerks and otherwise, has reserved, and does daily reserve to his collation generally and especially, as well archbishoprics, bishoprics, abbeys, and priories, as all other dignities and other benefices of England, which are of the advowson of people of Holy Church, and gives the same as well to aliens as to denizens, and takes of all such benefices the first-fruits, and many other profits, and a great part of the treasure of the said realm is carried away and dispended out of the realm by the purchasers of such graces aforesaid; and also by such privy reservations, many clerks, advanced in this realm by their true patrons, which have peaceably holden their advancements by long time, are suddenly put out; whereupon the said Commons have prayed our said lord the king, that since the right of the crown of England, and the law of the said realm is such, that upon the mischiefs and damages which happen to his realm, he ought, and is bound by his oath, with the accord of his people in his Parliament thereof, to make remedy for the removing of the mischief and damages which thereof ensue, that it may please him to ordain remedy therefore.

[*The king then reviews the case and decrees that*] all prelates and other people of Holy Church, which have advowsons of any benefices of the king's gift, or of any of his progenitors, or of other lords and donors, to do divine service, and other charges thereof ordained, shall have their collations and presentments freely to the same, in the manner as they were enfeoffed by their donors. [*If Rome does make a provision the king will intervene and take the revenues pending an election.*]

C. The Theory of Indulgences. Clement VI, Unigenitus Dei filius, *1343, from Walter Köhler,* Dokumente zum Ablassstreit (*Tübingen, 1934*).

The only begotten Son of God deigned to descend from the bosom of the Father into the womb of the Virgin in which and from which he conjoined the substance of our mortality with his divinity by an ineffable union in unity of person and this he did to redeem fallen humanity by making satisfaction to God the Father. . . . In order that the compassion of such an effusion might not be rendered vain, idle and superfluous the Holy Father, desiring to enrich His sons, acquired for the church militant a treasury that thus an infinite treasure might be available to men and that those who used it might be made partakers of the divine friendship. This treasure was not wrapped in a napkin, nor hidden in a field but was committed by the blessed Peter, the key bearer of heaven and his successors and vicars on earth that it should be dispensed to the healing of the faithful, for suitable and reasonable causes, now for the total and now for the partial remission of temporal penalty due for sins, whether generally or specially (as they deemed expedient to God) mercifully to be applied to those penitent and who had made confession. To this treasury the merits of the blessed Mother of God and of all the elect from the first just man to the very last are known to have been added. That this accumulation will be consumed or diminished is not in the least to be feared partly because of the infinite merits of Christ and partly because the more men are turned by its use to righteousness the more is the sum of the merits increased.

D. An Unstinting Hermit. In 1428 Henry VI granted a toll on all vessels entering the Humber for the maintenance of a light house which had been erected by a hermit, whose petition to the Commons for permission to proceed reads as follows. From Gordon Home, Yorkshire (A. & C. Black, London, 1908), p. 88.

                ✦   ✦   ✦

To the wyse Commones of this present Parlement. Besekith your povre bedemen, Richard Reedbarowe, Heremyte of the Chapell of our Lady and Seint Anne atte Ravensersporne. That forasmuche that many diverses straites and daungers been in the entryng into the river of Humbre out of the See, where ofte tymes by mysaventure many divers Vesselx, and Men, Godes and Marchaun-

dises, be lost and perished, as well by Day as be Night, for
defaute of a Bekyn, that shuld teche the people to hold in
the right chanell; so that the seid Richard, havyng compassion and pitee of the Cristen people that ofte tymes
are there perished . . . to make a Toure to be uppon day
light a redy Bekyn, whereyn shall be light gevyng by night,
to alle the Vesselx that comyn into the seid Ryver of
Humbre. . . .

IV. The Conciliar Period

A. The Decree of the Council of Constance, Sacrosancta,
April 6, 1415. Mirbt, No. 392.

✐   ✐   ✐

This holy synod of Constance first declares that it is
legitimately assembled in the Holy Spirit, that it constitutes a general council representing the Catholic Church,
that it has power immediately from Christ and that every
one of whatever status and dignity, even the papal is
bound to obey this council in those matters which pertain
to the faith, the extirpation of the said schism and the
reformation of the Church in head and members. Again
it is declared that any one of whatever status or condition,
even the papal, who contumaciously contemns the man-
dates, statutes, ordinances or precepts of this sacred synod
or any other general council legitimately assembled . . .
unless he repent shall be subject to condign penance and
shall be duly punished, if need be by recourse to other
arms of the law.

B. The decree Frequens, *Oct. 9, 1417. Mirbt, No. 393.*

✐   ✐   ✐

The frequent meeting of general councils is the best culture of the field of the Lord which roots out brambles,
thorns and thistles of heresy, error and schism, corrects
excesses, reforms deformity and restores the vineyard of
the Lord to an abundant fertility. The neglect of councils
has the reverse effect as the records of times past and
present abundantly display before our eyes. Therefore by
perpetual edict we enact, decree and ordain that general
councils from now on shall be celebrated thus: the first

shall follow immediately after five years from the closing of the present council, the second seven years after the close of the first and thereafter every ten years in places to be designated by the supreme pontiff a month before the close of each council with the approval and consent of the council or, if the pontiff is not available, by the designation of the council itself that by continuous sessions or their expectation the council may continually operate, which periods may be abbreviated by the supreme pontiff with the consent of his brethren the cardinals but under no circumstances shall be extended.

V. Sectarianism Tinged with Nationalism

A. Excerpts from Wyclif, modernized from Wyclif Select English Writings, *ed. Herbert E. Winn (Oxford, 1929), pp. 71, 86, 97, 124, 123.*

✓   ✓   ✓

Contrast of Christ and Antichrist, the Pope: Christ was most poor man from his birth to his death and left worldly riches and [*went about*] begging, after the state of innocence; but Antichrist against this, from the time that he be made pope till the time that he be dead, here coveteth to be worldly rich and casteth by many shrewd ways how that he may thus be rich. Christ was most meek man and bad learn this of him, but men say that the pope is most proud man of earth and maketh lords to kiss his feet where Christ washed his apostles' feet. Christ was most homely [*lowly*] man in life, in deed and in word; men say that this pope is not next to Christ in this, for where Christ went on his feet both to cities and little towns, they say this pope will be closed in a castle with great array. Where Christ came to John Baptist to be baptized of him, the pope sendeth after men to come to him wherever he be. Well I read that Saint Peter dwelled in a courier's house, but I read not of cardinal nor page that he had with him.

The Eucharist: I believe, as Christ and his apostles have taught us, that the sacrament of the altar, white and round, and like to other bread, is very God's body in form of bread. And therefore Saint Paul names it never but when he calls it bread. And right as it is heresy to believe that

Christ is a spirit and no body, so it is heresy to believe that this sacrament is God's body and no bread; for it is both together.

Predestination: So as Peter in his first fishing took two manner of fishes, some dwelled in the net and some burst the net and went away; so here in this Church been some ordained to bliss and some to pain, even if they live justly for a time. And so men say commonly that there been here two manner churches, holy Church or Church of God, that on no manner may be damned, and the church of the fiend, that for a time is good, and lasteth not; and this was never holy Church, nor part thereof.

The pope neither infallible, nor as such predestined, nor the head of the Church: Well I wot that these popes may err and sin, as Peter did, and yet Peter dreamed not thus, to show that men been saints in heaven. But it may befall that many men that been canonized by these popes been deep damned in hell, for they deceive and been deceived. Affirm we not as belief that if a man be chosen pope, then he is chosen to bliss, as he is here called "Blessed Father." And many believe that by their works they been deepest damned in hell. A heresy that cometh of this deceiveth many simple men, that if the pope determine ought, then it is sooth and to believe. But Lord, whether each pope be more and better with God than was Peter? But he erred oft and sinned much.

And if thou say that Christ's Church must have an head here in earth, sooth it is, for Christ is head, that must be here with his Church unto the day of doom. And if thou say that Christ must needs have such a vicar here in earth, deny thou Christ's power, and make this fiend above Christ.

B. 1. John Hus on the church of the predestined. Tractatus de Ecclesia, *ed. S. Harrison Thomson (Un. Col., 1946), §§ Ib, IIIe, VIIa, VIII, XVc.*

✓   ✓   ✓

There is one church of the sheep, another of the goats, one of the saints, another of the reprobates.

Just as in the case of the body there are waste materials so also in the church there are those who are not of the

Church. The tares stand together with the wheat. There are some who are in the Church in name and in fact as the predestined Catholics obedient to Christ, some neither in name nor in fact as the pagans, some only in name as the hypocrites, some in fact though not in name because condemned by the satraps of Antichrist.

It remains to be considered whether the Roman church is the holy apostolic Catholic Church, the bride of Christ, Boniface in the bull *Unam Sanctam* said yes and concluded that it is necessary for every human being to be subject to the Roman pontiff. Against this may be said, that the Roman church is a church whose head is the pope and whose body the cardinals but this church is not the holy apostolic Church because the pope and the cardinals have often been stained by error and sin. Take the case of the female pope Joanna [*legendary*]. The same may be said of many other popes who were heretics and deposed because of many enormities. The case is not proved by the *Donation of Constantine,* the deference shown by the emperor to the pope or by the requirement that every Christian take his case on pain of damnation to the most Holy Father. That the pope and the cardinals are the holy Catholic apostolic Church against which the gates of hell shall not prevail I cannot believe unless I receive a special divine revelation.

If the pope and the cardinals have scandalized Christian believers by pompous equipage, resplendent attire, exquisite and marvelous display, by inordinate craving for benefices and manifest ambition for honor exceeding that of the laity, shall they remain in the rulership of the universal Church as the manifest and true successors in office of the apostle Peter and the other apostles of Christ?

B. 2. Hus on the efficacy of unworthy priests. Tractatus Responsivus, *ed. S. Harrison Thomson* (*Princeton, 1937*). *pp. 1-7.*

⚡   ⚡   ⚡

Articles have been brought to me from the monastery of Rockycany which certain doctors have condemned. The first is that it is not an error to believe that the supreme pontiff does not have the plentitude of power in those matters which pertain to his administration and that if he be in mortal sin he does not have the power to bind and loose.

In the first epistle of John we read that to those who received him to them gave he the power to become the sons of God. This power meritoriously to edify and spiritually feed is given only to true, not feigned lovers of Christ. From which it follows that no one in mortal sin has such power meritoriously to feed spiritually the sheep of Christ or himself. No simoniac, no concubinous priest, worshipper of idols, no perverse vicar, false pope or cardinals, lovers of the world, false promissors of indulgences, hypocrites, covetous and carnal clerics, addicted to mortal crimes, exalting their own traditions and contemning the law of Christ have any such power. Therefore it is not erroneous or heretical to say that he who in these days is called the supreme pontiff or any other bishop or priest, being in mortal sin, does not have the power or authority or license or the knowledge given to exercise the keys of binding and loosing with regard to the faithful in the Church.

This, however, is to be noted that there is another variety of power which the scholastics call the power of orders, which the cleric enjoys for the administration of the sacraments so as to be spiritually beneficial to himself and to the laity. This power is established through a divine supernatural virtue from on high, which is not subject to the will of men according to the acceptance of persons. This power God sometimes confers by a sensible sign as He does by sacramental unction so that grace is conveyed through the sacrament of baptism, the Eucharist or any other of the sacraments.

— Reading No. 9 —

CHANGING VIEWS ON RELIGION AND THE CHURCH

I. The Church

A. William of Ockham on the impossibility of localizing authority in the Church. Dialogus, *Lyons, 1494, passages from Liber V and Liber VI, especially VI, xxxii. A dialog between a master and a disciple.*

✓   ✓   ✓

D. All Christians seem to agree that the total multitude of Christians cannot be heretical. Some say further that a general council cannot err, some that the Roman Church cannot; some again the college of cardinals is inerrant. Finally there are those who say that the pope cannot be polluted by heretical pravity. Now I desire that you show me what Christians think on this matter, and first whether it is possible that a pope canonically elected cannot err. *M.* On this point there are contrary opinions. Some assert that a pope canonically elected is capable of pertinacious heretical pravity, others the contrary. . . . That the pope canonically elected can diverge from the Catholic truth is proved by many examples. Paul said that Peter erred and resisted him to his face (Gal. 2).
D. The modern doctors will not admit that Peter ever erred.
M. Yes, Aquinas does. The modern doctors think that Peter erred, though not that he was a pertinacious heretic. Further examples are Marcellinus, Liberius, Anastasius II, Sylvester II, who made a pact with the devil, and latterly John XXII, who has denied the poverty of Christ and the apostles, contrary to the bull of Nicholas III.

D. Whether the college of cardinals can be stained by heretical pravity?

M. True, Christ said that the faith would remain to the end of the world but he did not say that with reference to any particular college established by the chief pontiff. A college which the pope can disband cannot be the Church which is not able to err, because the Church which is not able to err is not able not to be. Christ told this Church that he would be with her always, even unto the end of the world (Mt. 28:20). This Church did not have a beginning after the time of the apostles, as the college of cardinals did.

D. Whether the apostolic Roman see can err.

M. What is true of the whole is not necessarily true of each part. The whole Church cannot err, but the Roman church is only a part of the whole Church.

D. Can a general council err?

M. A general council is only a part of the Church militant.

D. And the entire body of the clergy?

M. Yes, the entire body of the clergy is not the whole Church.

D. What, then, of the entire multitude of men whether clerical or lay?

M. They may all be wrong and the Catholic faith conserved only by women. The reason is that the Church militant is one. There is no plurality of churches militant. But the multitude of men is not that one sole Church. If men constituted the whole of that Church no woman would be saved, for no person on this earthly pilgrimage can be saved without being a member of that Church. There is no reason to assume that the multitude of men cannot err unless it be supposed that the wisdom of men is greater than that of women or that men excel in piety. Of course only men can celebrate at the altar but we have already seen that this does not carry inerrancy since all the clergy can be in error, and if that be so then the whole body of the men can be heretical.

B. Marsilius of Padua on Dominium *and* usus, *from the text edited by C. W. Previté-Orton (Cambridge, England, 1928). Dictio II, Cap. xii-xiv, with slight paraphrasing to carry over the thought.*

✓   ✓   ✓

Strictly defined *dominium* has reference to the power of one who does not wish anything without his consent to be alienated to another. . . . Now we must distinguish between the rich and the poor. Rich is applied to those who have a superabundance or at least a sufficiency, poor to those who lack a superabundance or even necessities. Again there are the voluntary poor who renounce all temporal goods. Now let us consider the state of poverty called evangelical perfection, and how it was practised by Christ and the apostles. Here we must bear in mind that something permitted by human law may be forbidden by divine law. The perfect are not permitted by divine law to have recourse to human law to defend their right. Therefore they cannot exercise *dominium* which involves the right of vindication. But the use of a thing is not interdicted because to renounce this would be a form of homicide. He who would not make any use of things material would kill himself by hunger, cold or thirst. A distinction is thus to be made between the simple use and the above mentioned *dominium* which is the right of vindicating or prohibiting a thing or something appertaining thereunto.

Now I will show that it is possible to have the legitimate use of something and to use it up with the consent of him who exercises the *dominium* but without having the *dominium* oneself. At the outset we are to recognize that poverty arising from a voluntary renunciation is a virtue. It must be spontaneous because there is no virtue simply in being poor. The sum of it consists in a vow of reunuciation for Christ with readiness to suffer privation and need, to divest oneself of all holdings, private or common, giving up all legally acquired right of vindication of temporal goods in a coercive court of law. This means that no one dedicated to perfection can hold immobile goods, such as a house or a field, unless it be just long enough to sell it and give the money to the poor. To this it may be objected that if the bishops and priests were to follow this way of perfection they would have nothing with which to supply the future needs of the poor. Yes, but they do have a sort of *dominium* over the use of consumables, though some one else has the *dominium* over the source of these goods and without his consent, the use cannot be legitimately exercised.

The clergy themselves are entitled to daily food and

raiment. They may be supported by the tithe. If it is not adequate they can work at something else as Paul did at tent making. If it is more than adequate they are not to demand it. The successors of Christ and the apostles, dedicated to perfection, should not acquire fields, villas and castles. Although the early bishops did have fields they did not have the right of vindicating them in a court of law.

Some one will now ask, Whose then is this *dominium* over temporal goods, especially the immovable, that is the power of vindicating before a civil judge with coercive power, seeing that this *dominium* is interdicted to the ministers of the gospel dedicated to perfection? We reply that the *dominium* of the temporal goods which are marked for the support of the evangelical ministers resides with the *legislator* or his deputies, or with the patrons of ecclesiastical foundations.

II. Fideism

A. Ockham on the Trinity. Sent. *Q.I,* Dist. *XXV L-P and* Dist. *XXVI G and* Dist. *XXX, Q.IV Γ.*

✦   ✦   ✦

If it be said that persons constitute something common, and that being so there is a universal in divinity, I reply that the name person does not signify anything common but it signifies the many of which any particular may be an example, just as man does not signify anything common to all men but signifies simply all men. And if it be said that at least a universal is there, I say no. . . . Person is common to three persons but it is not a universal although the concept abstractable from the divine persons is common to the three persons, yet it does not have the character of a universal. The names of genera and species, such as man and animal, point to what their natures have in common, not to a common nature. They signify individuals in general. Similarly this word person does not signify an individual on the score of nature but of things subsisting in such a nature. In the case of the divine persons there is something in common. But this common element exists only in the mind and not beyond. If then it be asked what is common to the three persons I say that the community in reality is not such that any essence is common to the three persons. A community lies in words only and concepts in the same way that many may be said to constitute a whole.

Nevertheless that one essence is in reality these three relations is as easy to assume as that three absolutes are in reality distinct and nevertheless that one essence is in reality three absolutes.

In divine matters there is no such relation distinct in some fashion from all absolutes—nevertheless it is possible to concede that God is in reality Father and in reality Son, as it is conceded that God is in reality creating. But according to this way it ought to be assumed that in God there would be three absolutes in reality distinct.

B. Pietro Pomponazzi and the question of Immortality. De Immortalitate Animae, *facsimile ed. Wm. Henry Hay (Haverford, Penn., 1938)*, Cp. XV.

✓   ✓   ✓

All of this being so it seems to me that the course of wisdom is to regard the question of the immortality of the soul as a neutral problem comparable to that of the eternity of the world. So far as I can see there are no natural reasons compelling belief in the immortality of the soul, nor are there any proving the contrary, as many doctors who believe in the immortality of the soul have pointed out. For this reason I do not feel it incumbent upon me to record all the replies which others have adduced, notably the divine Thomas, who has spoken to this point clearly, gravely and fully. Therefore, we say with Plato, in the first book of The Laws, that to speak with certainty about anything on which many do not agree is something for God only. Since, then, in this matter so many illustrious men are at variance I do not see how the question can be resolved other than by God. At the same time it is highly inexpedient that man should lack such certitude. For if he is not sure he will have no positive goal for his action, since if the soul is immortal, then the things of earth are to be despised, and the eternal are to be pursued, but if mortal then the contrary. On which account I say that before the advent of grace God settled the question in diverse ways through the prophets and by supernatural signs, as appears plainly in the Old Testament. Now in these last days "He has spoken unto us through his Son, whom he appointed heir of all things, through whom also he made the worlds" (Heb. 1:2). He is true God and true man. He alone is truly the light by which all things are seen. He has made manifest by word and deed that the soul is immortal. By word, when he threatened eternal fire to the bad and promised reward to the good; by deed, when on the third day he arose from the dead . . . By as much as light excels that which is lighted, and truth surpasses the true and infinity the finite, by so much more has Christ demonstrated the immortality of the soul. Consequently the reasons which appear to disprove it are false. . . . On this and all points I submit to the judgment of the apostolic see. Finished by me, P.P., on the 24th day of September, 1516, in the fourth year of the Pontificate of Leo X to the praise of the undivided Trinity.

III. Mysticism

A. Eckhart. Meister Eckeharts Traktat "Von Abgeschiedenheit," *ed. Eduard Schaefer (Bonn, 1956), pp. 214-217.*

✓   ✓   ✓

The masters greatly laud love, as St. Paul said, "If I have not love I am nothing," but I would place detachment above love, because loves causes me to love God whereas detachment causes God to love me. Others again rate humility above all virtues but I place detachment higher because there can be humility without detachment, but not detachment without humility. You may ask then what is detachment if it be so excellent. Know, then, that true detachment is nothing other than that the spirit should be immovable before all the vicissitudes of love and suffering, honor, disgrace and shame, like a mountain of lead against a breeze. This immoveable detachment brings men into the greatest likeness with God because the fact that God is God comes from his immoveable detachment. You may ask whether Christ had this detachment when he cried, "My soul is troubled even unto death," or Mary in her lamentations before the cross, but here we must distinguish between the inner and the outward man. . . . Now I would inquire what is the object of pure detachment. To this I would say that it is neither this nor that. Detachment stands on a pure nothing. . . . Further I inquire what is the prayer of the detached heart? To this I answer and affirm that detached purity cannot pray. Because he who prays asks something from God. The detached heart desires nothing and has nothing of which it would be free. Dionysius says that all contestants run for a crown and this race is nothing other than a withdrawal from all that is created and a union of the soul with the uncreated. In this state the soul loses its own name. God draws her unto himself, so that in herself she becomes nothing just as the sun draws the dawn into himself that she becomes naught. When this detachment reaches the highest perfection then it becomes from knowledge ignorance, from love lovelessness, from light darkness. . . . The faster man flees from the creature the faster he is sought by the Creator. Detachment purifies the soul, purges the conscience, kindles the heart, awakens the spirit, extinguishes desires, makes God known, eliminates the creatures and effects union with God. Now understand, the swiftest steed to bring you to this perfection is suffering, for none experiences greater eternal sweetness than those who endure with Christ in greatest bitterness. The most solid foundation on which this perfection rests is humility. He who would attain perfect detachment must seek perfect humility by which he may come to the closest proximity to the Godhead. May He help us thereto, who is the highest detachment, that is God Himself. Amen.

B. Tauler. The sermons of Tauler still present a problem as to their authenticity. Modern critical editions accept only those for which there is strong manuscript evidence. The following excerpts do not qualify, because the first two are from the Basel edition of 1521 and the third from the Cologne edition of 1543. Nevertheless, they do represent late medieval German mysticism. The translation is by Susanna Winkworth The History . . . of . . . John Tauler (*London, 1857; New York, 1858*).

✓   ✓   ✓

Third Sunday in Advent. Again, a spiritual life may be fitly called a wilderness, by reason of the many sweet flowers which spring up and flourish where they are not trodden under foot by man. In this respect the life of one dead to the world may well be likened to a wilderness, seeing that so many virtues may be learned by continual and earnest striving; but because the effort needed is toilsome and painful at the first, few are willing to make it. In this wilderness are found the lilies of chastity, and the white roses of innocence; and therein are found, too, the red roses of sacrifice, when flesh and blood are consumed in the struggle with sin, and the man is ready, if need be, to suffer martyrdom,—the which is not easily to be learned in the world. In this wilderness, too, are found the violets of humility, and many other fair flowers and wholesome roots, in the examples of holy men of God. And in this wilderness shalt thou choose for thyself a pleasant spot wherein to dwell; that is, a holy life, in which thou mayest follow the example of God's saints in pureness of heart, poverty of spirit, true obedience, and all other virtues; so that it may be said, as it is in the Canticles: "Many flowers have appeared in our land"; for many have died full of holiness and good works.

Thursday in Easter week: First, I say God rewards nothing but love. By three things may a man win reward: by outward acts, by inward contemplation, and by inward aspiration and love. The outward act has no merit unless it be wrought in love: for the outward act perishes and is over, and cannot merit that which is eternal. . . . In the second place, I said that God only rewards out of love. For from the love wherewith He loveth man, He giveth Himself, He giveth His very self as a reward, He giveth Himself wholly, and not in part; for God hath loved man with an eternal love, and He gives a man nothing less than Himself.

In the third place, He rewards a man with love. For this reward consists in being able to behold God in His clearness without a veil, and to enjoy the fruition of His love, and keep it for all eternity.

First Sunday after Easter: A pure heart is more precious in the sight of God than aught else on earth. A pure heart is a fair, fitly-adorned chamber, the dwelling of the

Holy Ghost, a golden temple of the Godhead; a sanctuary of the only-begotten Son, in which He worships the Heavenly Father; an altar of the grand, divine sacrifice, on which the Son is daily offered to the Heavenly Father; a treasury of divine riches; a storehouse of divine sweetness; the reward of all the life and sufferings of Christ.

C. The Imitation of Christ *traditionally attributed to Thomas à Kempis, translated from* Thomae Hemerken a Kempis Opera Omnia *I-II, ed. M. I. Pohl (Freiburg i. Br., 1910).*

Ch. I. Of what value will it be to you to dispute loftily of the Trinity if you lack humility and thereby displease the Trinity? Truly, lofty words do not make a man holy and righteous, but a virtuous life makes a man dear to God. I would rather feel compunction than to know its definition. If you were to know the whole Bible by rote and all the maxims of the philosophers, of what use would all this be apart from the love and peace of God? Vanity of vanities, and all is vanity except to love God and to serve him only.

Ch. II. Much better is a poor peasant who serves God than a philosopher who, unmindful of himself, contemplates the courses of the stars.

Ch. III. What profit is there in great disputation about hidden and obscure matters for the which we shall not be condemned in the judgment because we know them not? O Truth, who art God, make me to know thee in everlasting love. Often I am weary of reading and hearing many things. In thee alone is all that I crave and desire. Let all doctors be silent and all creatures hold their peace in thy sight. Speak thou only unto me. The more one is united with thee and made simple within, the more does one understand high things without striving, for one receives the light of knowledge which comes down from above. . . . A humble acquaintance with one self is a more certain way to God than a profound inquiry after knowledge.

Ch. XI. Many there are who follow Jesus in the breaking of the bread, but few up to the drinking of the cup of the passion.

— Reading No. 10 —

RENAISSANCE RELIGION AND PREMONITIONS OF REFORM

I. The Dignity of Man. Pico della Mirandola. De Hominis Dignitate, *ed. E. Garin (Florence, 1942), translation of excerpts from pp. 104-124.*

✦ ✦ ✦

The Supreme Father, God the Architect, having already used up all the forms in the creation of the world, wondered what special distinction was left for Him to confer upon man. He decided that man's singularity should consist in his freedom to participate in all of the forms. Wherefore God addressed Adam: "We have conferred upon you, O Adam, no certain seat, no proper form, no peculiar function, that you might opt what seat, what form, what functions you perfer, to have and to hold by your will and choice. Others have their nature prescribed by Our laws, but you may set your own bonds with no constriction, in accord with your arbitriment in whose hand I have placed you. I have set you in the middle of the world that you may the better survey what is in the world. We have made you neither celestial nor terrestrial, neither mortal nor immortal, in order that as a free and sovereign modeler and sculptor, as it were, you may fashion yourself into the form which you prefer. You are able to degenerate into the lower forms, which are the brutes, and to regenerate yourself by your own volition into the higher, which are divine."

O supreme liberality of God the Father, O supreme and admirable felicity of man! Let us then mount above all that is on the earth to the supramundane court which is closest to the most eminent divinity. There, as the sacred mysteries relate the Seraphim, Cherubim and Thrones have their places. The Seraph burns with the fire of love, the Cherub is refulgent with the splendor of intelligence, the Throne is established on the stability of judgment. . . . Let us inquire of Paul, that elect vessel, what he saw the Cherubim doing when he was rapt to the third heaven. He will respond by the mouth of Dionysius, his interpreter: to be purged, to be illuminated, to be perfected. We ascend first by the ladder of philosophy. She is able to allay the dissensions which vex, distress and lacerate the mind distraught, yet only in such fashion as to remind us of the dictum of Heraclitus that nature is born to strife. Therefore the true quiet and the solid peace are the reward and privilege of her mistress, most holy theology. As the Master says when he sees us struggling, "Come unto me all ye that labor, come and I will refresh you. Come and I will give you the peace which the world cannot give" (Mt. 11:28; John 14:27).

Since we are called with such tenderness, since we are invited with such graciousness, let us with winged feet like terrestrial Mercuries, fly up to the embrace of the Most Blessed Mother to enjoy the peace desired, the peace most holy, the union indissoluble, the friendship of accord in which all souls accord not only in that one mind which is above every mind, but in an ineffable manner are fused into one. Finally comes the vision through the light of theology. Who would not desire to be initiated into these rites? Who transcending the earthly, despising the goods of fortune, forgetting the body, would not desire, while still on earth, to be a companion of the gods, inebriated with the nectar of eternity, to receive being mortal the gift of immortality? Who would not wish to be seized by the frenzy of Socrates, that sped by the oars of winged feet he might ascend most rapidly from this evil world to the new Jerusalem? Be seized, fathers, be seized with the Socratic frenzies, which place us out of our minds and set ourselves and our minds in God. . . . Then Bacchus, the leader of the Muses, showing to us who pursue philosophy the invisible things of God through his mysteries, that is the visible signs of nature, will intoxicate us from the richness of the divine abode in which if we be faithful like Moses, holy theology will animate us with a double fury. Then lifted to eminent

height we shall measure from eternity all that was and is
and is to be, beholding their primordial beauty. As seers
of Phoebus we shall be winged lovers, rapt by an ineffable
love, stung as by a barb, like flaming Seraphim we shall
be beyond ourselves, full of God. We shall be no longer
ourselves, but rather He who made us.

II. Religious Tolerance

*A. Nicholas of Cusa. De Pace Fidei, Opera Omnia VII,
ed. Raymond Klibansky and Hildebrand Bascour (Hamburg,
1949), partly translated, partly paraphrased.*

✓   ✓   ✓

When once the Turks were fiercely persecuting the
Christians at Constantinople an ardent soul implored the
Almighty to allay the dissension over religion. God then
carried him to a council in heaven, where a priest ap-
pealed to the Almighty saying, "O Lord of the universe,
Thou art a God who hidest Thyself [*deus absconditus*].
Be gracious unto us and disclose Thyself. Save Thy peo-
ple. Let us know how there may be one religion with a
diversity of rites, if such diversity cannot be overcome."
God replied that He had done His best by sending His
Son, but Christ proposed a council of faith at Jerusalem.
In attendance there were Catholic Christians: Italian,
German, Spanish and English; non-Catholics: Greek, Bo-
hemian, Armenian and Chaldean; non-Christians: Arab,
Turk, Jew, Persian and Tartar. Their questions are an-
swered now by Christ the Word, now by Peter, now by
Paul.

Greek: It will be difficult to wean each nation from the
faith defended by its blood.

The Word: Are we agreed that there is only one wisdom?

Arab: We are agreed that we should seek wisdom, but
what of polytheists?

The Word: Belief in many gods presupposes belief in divinity.

Indian: What of images?

The Word: They do no harm unless God is supposed to
dwell in stones.

Arab: What of the Trinity?

The Word· The names applied to God are the inventions

of men. God in Himself is ineffable. But in His unity is diversity.

Peter entering: Does not almost every religion, Jew, Christian and Arab believe in immortality? How then can they be immortal if they do not adhere in indissoluble union?

German: But they are not agreed as to the nature of the blessed life. The Jews expect temporal blessings, the Arabs, carnal delights.

Peter: Avicenna prefers the intellectual felicity of the vision and fruition of God.

Tartar: How about circumcision, baptism, etc.?

Paul entering: We are not saved by works, but by faith, though we must keep the commandments.

Tartar: Yes, but the Jews take the commandments of Moses, the Arabs those of Mohammed, the Christians of Christ.

Paul: The commandments, are few, clear and common to all.

Englishman: What of diverse rites?

Paul: Devotion may be increased by vying in zeal.

Then the King of Kings decreed that under the names to which they were accustomed all should hold one faith in perpetual peace.

B. Thomas More on Religious Liberty in Utopia. From the English translation of the Utopia *by Ralph Robynson in 1551, ed. J. H. Lupton (Oxford, 1895). From Chapter IX.*

✓   ✓   ✓

There be dyuers kyndes of religion, not only in sondry partes of the Llande, but also in dyuers places of euery citie. . . . But the moste and wysest parte . . . beleue that there is a certayne Godlie powre unknowen, euerlastyng, incromprehansible, inexplicable, farre aboue the capacitie and retche of mans witte, dispersed through out all the worlde, not in bygnes, but in vertue and powre. Hym they call the father of all. . . . They also, whiche do not agree to Christes religion, feare [*deter*] no man frome it, nor speake agaynste anye man that hath receyued it. Sauing that one of oure companye in my presence was sharpely punished. He, as sone as he was baptised, began

against our willes, with more earnest affection then wis-
dome, to reason of Christes religion; and began to waxe
so hotte in his matter, that he dyd not only preferre oure
relygion before all other, but also dyd vtterlye despise an
condempne al other, callynge them prophane, and the
followers of them wicked and deuelishe, and the chyldren
of euerlasting dampnation. When he had thus long rea-
soned the matter, they layde holde of hym, accused hym,
and condempned hym into exyle; not as a despyser of religion, but as a sedicious persone, and a rayser vp of dissention amonge the people. . . . Kyng Vtopus . . .
haering that the inhabitauntes of the lande were before
his comyng thether at contynuall dissention and stryfe
among themselfes for their religions; . . . made a decrie,
that it shoulde be lawfull for euery man to fauoure and
followe what religion he would, and that he myght do the
best he cold to bryng other to his opinion; so that he dyd
it peaceably, gentelye, quyetly, and soberlye, without
hastye and contentious rebuking and inuehyng against
other. If he coulde not by fayre and gentle speche induce
them vnto his opinion, yet he should vse no kinde of violence, and refrayne from displeasaunt and seditious
woordes. To him that would vehemently and feruently in
this cause striue and contend, was decreid bannishment or
bondage.

This lawe did kynge Vtopus make, not only for the
maintainance of peace . . . but also because he thought
this decrye whuld make for the furtheraunce of religion.
. . . Furthermore though there be one religion whiche
alone is trew . . . yet did he well forsee that the trewthe
of the [its] owne powre woulde at the laste issue owte and
come to lyght. . . . Therefore he gaue to euery man free
libertie and choyse to beleue what he woulde; sauinge
that he earnestly and straytelye chardged them, that no
man shoulde conceaue so vile and base an opinion of
the dignitie of mans nature, as to thinke that the sowles
do dye and perishe with the bodye; or that the worlde
runneth at al auentures, gouerned by no diuine proui-
dence.

C. *Erasmus.* Adversus Monachos quosdam Hispanos
(*1528*), Opera *IX, 1056A, 1057D. My own translation*

in Castellio Concerning Heretics (*New York, 1935*), *pp. 33-34.*

✓   ✓   ✓

The ancients philosophized very little about divine things. The curious subtlety of the Arians drove the orthodox to greater necessity. Let the ancients be pardoned, but what excuse is there for us, who raise so many curious, not to say impious, questions about matters far removed from our nature? We define so many things which may be left in ignorance or in doubt without loss of salvation. Is it not possible to have fellowship with the Father, Son, and Holy Spirit without being able to explain philosophically the distinction between them and between the nativity of the Son and the procession of the Holy Ghost? If I believe the tradition that there are three of one nature, what is the use of labored disputation? If I do not believe, I shall not be persuaded by any human reasons. You will not be damned if you do not know whether the Spirit proceeding from the Father and the Son has one or two beginnings, but you will not escape damnation, if you do not cultivate the fruits of the Spirit which are love, joy, peace, patience, kindness, goodness, long-suffering, mercy, faith, modesty, continence and chastity. The sum of our religion is peace and unanimity, but these can scarcely stand unless we define as little as possible, and in many things leave each free to follow his own judgment, because there is great obscurity in many matters, and man suffers from this almost congenital disease that he will not give in when once a controversy is started, and after he is warmed up he regards as absolutely true that which he began to sponsor quite casually. Many problems are now reserved for a general council. It would be better to defer questions of this sort to the time when no longer in a glass darkly we see God face to face. Formerly, faith was in life rather than in the profession of creeds. Presently, necessity required that articles be drawn up, but only a few with apostolic sobriety. Then the depravity of the heretics exacted a more precise scrutiny of the divine books. When faith came to be in writings rather than in hearts, then there were almost as many faiths as men. Articles increased and sincerity decreased. Contention grew hot and love grew cold. The doctrine of Christ, which at first knew no hairsplitting, came to depend on the aid of philosophy. This was the first stage in the fall of the Church. The injection of the authority of the emperor into this affair did not greatly aid the sincerity of faith. When faith is in the mouth rather than in the heart, when the solid knowledge of Sacred Scripture fails us, nevertheless by terrorization we drive men to believe what they do not believe, to love what they do not love, to know what they do not know. That which is forced cannot be sincere, and that which is not voluntary cannot please Christ.

III. Historical Criticism. Lorenzo Valla, Calumnia theologica Laurentio Vallensi . . . intentata, quo negasset symbolum membratim articulatimque per Apostolos esse compositum (*Strasburg, 1522*), *Aiij.*

✓   ✓   ✓

A few days ago a certain Brother Antonio Bentontio of the Friars Minor came to Rome bawling, or shall I say bellowing egregiously. I fell in as he was teaching the creed to a throng of boys telling them that Peter said, "I believe in God the Father almighty"; Andrew: "maker of heaven and earth," and so on for the rest of the apostles. I tackled him and asked who ever heard that the creed was given article by article by the apostles. "The doctors of the Church," he answered. "Which ones?" I countered. "The doctors approved by the Church are Ambrose, Jerome, Augustine and Gregory." He snapped back that Bonaventura said so and he is as great as any of them. I told him that in matters subject to reason posterity is as good as antiquity, but when it comes to what happened in the past we can't pass over the testimony of those who lived in the past. Besides, just where is this found in Bonaventura? Some time later a Dominican, reputed to be an Inquisitor, demanded of me whether I believed the creed to have been given by the apostles. I told him I thought it came from the Nicene Council. He replied that this was heresy and unless I recanted he would damn me. I replied that I believed what Mother Church believes. "Revoke," he shouted. "Show me," I answered, "why this should be revoked." "Do you hold then to your opinion?" "Are you trying to change my mouth or my mind? What good will, it be if I confess with my mouth what I do not believe with my mind? I tell you I believe what Mother Church believes even if she doesn't know anything about it."

IV. Satire

A. Boccaccio on relics. Novelle IV, 10.

✔   ✔   ✔

Fra Cipolla of the order of St. Anthony was accustomed once a year in the month of August to visit a certain village to collect alms for his order. He was small, ruddy, merry and the jolliest rascal in the world, a marvelous talker who had he been educated would have rivalled Cicero or even Quintillian. Arriving on a Sunday morning he informed the villagers at mass they would assemble on the day following with their alms he would show them a feather of the Angel Gabriel which had been found in the chamber of the Virgin Mary after the annunciation. Two young wags in the throng resolved to play a trick on the friar and while he was at meat, having searched his saddle bags, found a little box wrapped in taffeta and inside a parrot feather. For this they substituted some coals. On the morrow the friar before a huge concourse eulogized the Angel Gabriel, unwrapped the taffeta, opened the box, saw the coals and without blinking went right on to say that before exhibiting the relic he must tell how he came by it and others. He had gone to Jerusalem and visited the Patriarch Dontblameme Anitpleaseyerighness, who had shown him a finger of the Holy Ghost, a forelock of the seraph that appeared to St. Francis, nail parings of one of the Cherubim, a rib of the Word made flesh, some vestments of the Holy Catholic Faith, some of the rays of the star which appeared to the Magi, an urn containing the sweat of St. Michael when he fought the devil, etc. The patriarch had given the friar a tooth of the Holy Cross, a box containing some of the sound of the bells in Solomon's temple, the feather aforementioned of the Angel Gabriel and some of the coals used to roast the blessed martyr St. Laurence. "These other relics," said the friar, "I have not been able to exhibit until now because they had not yet been certified, but now they have wrought miracles and may be displayed. I have not wanted to soil the feather of the Angel Gabriel by putting it in the same box with the coals of St. Laurence, and have kept them therefore in separate but almost identical boxes, easy to confuse. That is what has happened today, but God willed it so, because we are only two days from the feast of St. Laurence and God desired to enflame your hearts by the sight of these blessed coals extinguished by the sweat which the saint exuded during the roasting. If you are marked with the sign of the cross with one of these coals fire will not touch you for a year." As the people gathered about him he made the biggest possible crosses on the white smocks, doublets and veils, assuring the people that although the coals were being diminished they would be miraculously replenished. Thus he collected a much larger offering than usual. Before his departure the rogues, who had nearly cracked their jaws with laughing, returned the feather, which he used to good effect the next year.

B. Skit on the Inquisition. Crotus Rubeanus. Tractatulus quidam solemnis de arte et modo inquirendi. Hutteni Operum Supplementum *VI, ed. Boecking (Leipzig, 1864),* pp. 489-499.

✦　　　　✦　　　　✦

To the most reverend Fathers in Christ Sylvester Prierias, Master of the Sacred Palace and Jacob von Hochstraten, Inquisitor of Heretical Pravity in Germany, from a brother of the same order, greeting. In as much as in our time the seeds of heresy sprout and some say the Inquisitors don't know how to inquire, I have been moved to write on the method of inquiry, not to instruct you, but to show the asses how much better two such luminaries as yourselves could do, if a humble professor like me does so well. First it is necessary to invoke the Holy Ghost and secondly to believe that the pope cannot err, for he who questions this would not be an inquisitor, but should be inquired into, for to doubt is the same as not to believe according to Aristotle's *Physics*. Since the pope is the prelate of prelates he is consequently the church of the churches. This conclusion is deduced from the same by univocal definition. Armed with the whole armor of God the Inquisitor shall smile like a dog showing his teeth, contort his face, protrude his lips, and wave his arms with fingers outspread. If the heretic appeals to Scripture dismiss him with a mild derisive laugh, not an indecorous snort, for this matter must be handled in gravity and suavity in the Holy Ghost. If the Inquisitor is in danger of being drawn into a discussion of Scripture, from which he might emerge with confusion, let him stamp his feet, for a riot on behalf of the Church is meritorious if it proceed from the right intention according to Aristotle. If it be asked why no one was burned in the 1300 years before the Council of Constance, the answer is that in those days there were no Inquisitors. Had there been, I doubt whether Jerome, Augustine and Paul would have escaped. Lucky for you, Paul, that you lived before the minds of men were so keen!

V. Premonitions of Upheaval

A. Sebastian Brant, Narrenschyff, *ed. Hans Koegler (Basel, 1913),* Der Entschrist.

St. Peter's bark now lists and pitches.
I fear she will be food for fishes.
The waves are pounding at her ribs.
No wonder if her timber gives.
Seldom is the truth now heard,
For men pervert God's Holy Word,
Twist the Scriptures to their mind
And leave the truth of God behind.
Forgive me if your nose I grip.
Antichrist is in the ship. . . .
In closing let me this indite.
Our faith resembles much a light
When the wick is nigh to go,
Spits and sputters, burning low.
Seeing the like I'm bound to say
We're not far off the judgment day.

B. Geiler of Kaisersberg preaching before the Emperor Maximillian in 1510, reported in "The Chronicle of Daniel Specklin," Bulletin d. la Soc. pour la Conservation des

Monuments Historiques d'Alsace *II ser. vol. 14* (*Strasburg, 1889*), *p. 297.*

✓   ✓   ✓

Then at the end of his sermon Dr. Kaisersberg turned again to the question of reformation. Said he, "If the pope, the bishop, the emperor and the king do not reform our unspiritual, crazy, godless life, God will raise up a man to do it. I wish I might live to see the day and be his disciple, but I'm too old. But there are many of you here who will see and when that happens I bid you recall what I have said."

CHRONOLOGY

Jerome   340-420
Patrick   386-459
Clovis baptized   496
Gregory I, pope   590-604
Augustine's mission   597
Whitby, synod   664
Boniface   675-755
Pippin, Donation   754
Charlemagne crowned   800
Alcuin   735-804
Ansgar's mission   830
Nicholas I, pope   858-867
Cyril and Methodius ca. 863
Cluny founded   910
Vladimir baptized   987
Cardinals established   1059
Gregory VII   1073-1085
Jerusalem captured   1099
Anselm   1033-1109
Bernard   1091-1153
Abelard   1079-1142
Waldo, conversion   1173
Innocent III   1198-1216
Dominic   1170-1221
Francis   1182-1226
Innocent IV   1243-1254

Thomas Aquinas   1227-1274
Boniface VIII   1294-1303
Babylonian capt. 1305-1377
John XXII   1316-1334
Ockam   1270-1350
Marsilius   1290?-?1343
Scotus   1265?-1308
Eckhart   1260-1327
Tauler   1300-1361
Wyclif   1324-1384
Boccaccio wrote   1313
Constance council   1414-1418
Hus   1366-1415
Valla   1407-1457
Nicholas V   1447-1455
Thomas à Kempis   1380-1471
Cusa   1401-1464
Pomponazzi wrote   1416
Sixtus IV   1471-1484
Alexander VI   1492-1503
Julius II   1503-1513
Geiler   1445-1510
Crotus wrote   1515
Brant   1457?-1521

BIBLIOGRAPHY

SOURCES: Bibliography of Farrar and Evans (Columbia, 1946). COLLECTIONS:
H. Bettenson, *Documents of the Christian Church* (Christian Classics, 1943); B. J. Kidd, *Documents Illustrative of the History of the Church,* vol. III (1941); E. Henderson, *Historical Documents* (1910); N. Downs, *Basic Documents in Medieval History* (Anvil, 1959); A. Fremantle, *Age of Belief* (Mentor, 1955); Christian Classics, vols. X-XV, covering asceticism, scholasticism, mysticism, reform and Aquinas. Aquinas: *Truth of the Christian Faith* (Image, 1956); *Philosophical Texts* (Galaxy, 1960). Anselm: *Selections* (Philosophical Classics, 1935); *The Era of Charlemagne,* S. Easton and H. Wieruszowski (Anvil, 1961). LETTERS: Boniface and Gregory VII, ed. Emerton (1940 and 1932); Bernard, ed. B. S. James (1953).

MEDIEVAL CHURCH: W. R. Cannon, *Christianity in the Middle Ages* (1960); G. G. Coulton, *Five Centuries of Religion,* 4 vols. (1923-1950); C. Dawson, *Medieval Religion* (1934) and *Religion and the Rise of Western Culture* (1934); M. Deanesly, *Medieval Church* (1934).

EARLY MIDDLE AGES: E. Duckett, *Gateway to the Middle Ages* (1938), in 3 paperback vols. (Ann Arbor, 1961); H. Haskins, *Renaissance of the 12th Century* (Meridian, 1957); K. S. Latourette, *History of the Expansion of Christianity,* vol. II (1938); F. Lot, *End of the Ancient World* (Torchbook, 1961); H. O. Taylor, *Emergence of Christian Culture* (Torchbook, 1958); R. W. Southern, *Making of the Middle Ages* (Yale, 1961).

LATE MIDDLE AGES: A. Flick, *Decline of the Medieval Church,* 2 vols. (1930); J. Huizinga, *Waning of the Middle Ages* (Anchor, 1956); P. O. Kristeller, *Renaissance Thought* (*Torchbook,* 1961); L. Pastor, *History of the Popes,* 40 vols. (1891-1953).

BIOGRAPHY: St. Alcuin by E. Duckett (1951); St. Alfred by E. Duckett (1956); St. Bernard by W. W. Williams (1952); St. Dominic by B. Jarrett (1947); *Heloise and Abelard* by E. Gilson (Ann Arbor, 1960); St. Francis by L. Salvatorelli (1928); John Hus by M. Spinka (1941); Innocent III by J. Clayton (1941); Stephen Langton by F. M. Powicke (1928); John Wyclif by H. B. Workman, 2 vols. (1926).

CHURCH AND STATE: G. Barraclough, ed., *Medieval Germany* (1938); Z. N. Brooke, *Lay Investiture* (1939); N. F. Cantor, *Church Kingship* (1958); G. G. Coulton, *Inquisition* (1938); A. P. D'Entreves, *Medieval Contribution* (1939); L. Gabel, *Benefit of Clergy* (1928-1929); O. von Gierke, *Political Theories* (Beacon, 1958); H. C. Lea, *Inquisition,* 3 vols. (1922); S. Runciman, *Crusades,* 3 vols. (1951-1954) and *The Medieval Manichee* (Compass, 1961); G. Tellenbach, *Church and State* (1940); B. Tierney, *Conciliar Theory* (1955); W. Ullmann, *Medieval Papalism* (1949) and *Growth of Papal Power* (1955).

RELIGIOUS ORDERS: E. Davison, *Forerunners of St. Francis* (1927); D. Knowles, *Religious Orders in England*, 3 vols. (1948-1959); V. Scudder, *Franciscan Adventure* (1931); L. M. Smith, *Cluny* (1930).

RELIGIOUS LIFE: C. Butler, *Western Mysticism* (1923); B. L. Manning, *Peoples' Faith* (1919); G. R. Owst, *Preaching in Medieval England* (1926) and *Literature and Pulpit* (1933); W. A. Pantin, *English Church in the 14th Century* (1955); R. Petry, *No Uncertain Sound* (1947); F. M. Powicke, *Christian Life in the Middle Ages* (1935).

THEOLOGY AND PHILOSOPHY: in addition to the general treaments by Seeberg, Harnack and McGiffert: F. C. Copleston, *Medieval Philosophy* (Torchbook, 1961); M. De Wulf, *Philosophy and Civilization* (1922); E. Gilson, *Reason and Revelation* (1938); D. Hawkins, *Sketch of Medieval Philosophy* (1947); G. Leff, *Medieval Thought* (Penguin, 1958); H. Rashdall, *Universities of the Middle Ages*, 2 vols. (1895); P. Vignaux, *Philosophy in the Middle Ages* (Meridian, 1959).

ART: H. Adams, *Mont-Saint-Michel and Chartres* (Anchor, 1959); G. G. Coulton, *Art and the Reformation*, 2 vols. (Torchbook, 1958); J. Harvey, *Gothic England* (1947) and *Gothic World* (1950); E. Mâle, *Gothic Image* (Torchbook, 1958); C. R. Morey, *Medieval Art* (1942); E. Panofsky, *Abbot Suger* (1946); O. von Simson, *Gothic Cathedral* (1956); W. Worringer, *Form in Gothic* (1927).

INDEX